As The Shadows Lengthen

Sermons Preached On Special Occasions

Richard E. Boye

CSS Publishing Company, Inc., Lima, Ohio

AS THE SHADOWS LENGTHEN

Library of Congress Cataloging-in-Publication Data

Boye, Richard E., 1928-
    As the shadows lengthen : sermons preached on special occasions / Richard E. Boye.
      p.   cm.
    ISBN 0-7880-1795-0 (alk. paper)
    1. Occasional sermons. 2. Evangelical Lutheran Church in America—Sermons. 3. Sermons, American—20th century. I. Title.
BV4254.2 .B68 2001
252'.04135—dc21

00-065117
CIP

For more information about CSS Publishing Company resources, visit our website at www.csspub.com.

ISBN 0-7880-1795-0

Table Of Contents

Preface

There is something quite definite I have to say, and I have it so much upon my conscience that (as I feel) I *dare not die without having uttered it.* For the instant I die and thus leave this world (so I understand it) I shall in the very same second be infinitely far away, in a different place where still within the same second the question will be put to me: *"Hast thou uttered the definite message quite definitely?"* And if I have not done so, what then?

Soren Kierkegaard

Introduction

I am writing these words on a snowy Sunday afternoon in Radford, Virginia, more than six years after retiring from the active ministry. It has been a good time though not without its particular challenges. I am enjoying the freedom I now have out of the pressure-cooker of serving my last ten years as Senior Pastor in one of the largest churches in the Evangelical Lutheran Church in America. Facetiously, I used to call this congregation "The Church of Perpetual Meetings," and I often referred to the pressures I felt there as having guns — plural! — to the head. In this situation I always felt I had all-too-little time for creative thought and writing. I just did the best I could week by week as many of you reading these words are now doing and well understand.

Now, instead of preaching most Sundays, I sit in the pew of the congregation of which we are members. My wife and I have also had the opportunity we rarely had before to visit other congregations for worship. I like both of these opportunities. They offer me a true chance to worship God and to be concerned, as well I should be, for the spiritual growth of my *own* soul rather than having always to be consciously aware of all the details of church worship. Moreover, it is a *real joy* for me to be able to place in the offering plates our family offering *with my own hands*, something I was only rarely able to do during the forty-one and a half years I served as an active pastor.

Moreover, during these retirement years my dear wife and I have had some good leisurely visits with our four children, and we have even caught up on many personal and household things which we somehow could never tackle while actively engaged in parish work. We even found the time to build a house here in the mountains of Virginia and then move here from our beloved Minnesota lakeside home in order to be closer to our children. Yes, indeed! It has been a good time, though busier than I had anticipated, and I have enjoyed it. I am a happy man, still married to the girl of my dreams who is my best friend, and filled with life.

During these six retirement years, however, I have experienced an inner gnawing. More than half a century ago I stopped running away from God and answered the call of the Lord to the gospel ministry. My response was similar to that of Isaiah who answered God's call by saying, "Here am I; send me!" (6:8). Now as a *young* 71-year-old man, I still do not believe I have yet finished everything God has called me to do with the lifetime He has given me. Coupled with this is Saint Paul's admonition to Timothy: "Do not neglect the gift that is in you ..." (1 Timothy 4:14). I resonate, therefore, with something General Douglas MacArthur said in his final address to West Point cadets in 1962: "The shadows are lengthening for me. The twilight is here." With that thought — by no means an unhappy one for Heaven awaits me, I am sure — but with the thought that my days are running out, there are still some things I must say and I hope say them *"quite definitely."*

About three months into our retirement, we attended church with my daughter's family in Montana. The anthem that day, which deeply moved and motivated me, was titled, "Arise, O God, and Shine." Admittedly, that anthem was about God's coming being akin to a sunrise, but somehow as this theme filtered through into my soul it seemed as though God were saying to me: "Richard, what a waste if you, a retired preacher, don't somehow find ways to continue to serve Me and to share something of what the Spirit has given you as well as what you have learned along life's way." This book is an attempt to do just that.

Back in the 1940s, when the first wild, Spirit-implanted thoughts of the ministry were flitting through my life, my pastor in St. Louis, the late Reverend Dr. Frederick F. Mueller, would occasionally talk to me about the call of God. I "fought" him as indeed I was "fighting" God as well. Beyond the general feeling of unworthiness for such a high calling, my main argument was that I would quickly run out of things to say on Sunday morning. I told Dr. Mueller that with a bit of good fortune I just might be able to make it through the first 52 Sundays with something to say, but beyond that I would be left *sermonless.* I was wrong! *Across all these years the Holy Spirit has never ceased to inspire me. He has given me insight into Scripture, put themes into my mind and heart, and often given me words faster than I could type or preach them.* The truth is that the Bible is so intertwined with life and life is so intertwined with the Bible that, with the boost of the Spirit of God, the wellspring of sermon-making will *never* run dry. I offer this thought as an encouragement for young fledgling preachers.

Here I am in the year 2000, therefore, after more than five decades of preaching, and I have not yet run out of sermons. I recognize now that I will never be able to get to all the biblical themes I had hoped one day to preach on and for which I have boxes of notes and folders that will never find their way into a sermon. If I cannot ever do all I had once hoped, however, I *can* choose to do that which I am able, which is why these sermons have been preached and why this book is being written.

Only three of the nineteen sermons in this book were preached prior to my retirement. Including my farewell sermon at my final parish, Elim Lutheran Church in Robbinsdale, Minnesota, fourteen of these sermons were preached after retirement. Two of these sermons have not been preached, and one of them was never intended to be preached as will become clear as you read it. These particular sermons instead were meant to be read and pondered. Some of these sermons were preached to large congregations, but I am just as happy to say that seven of them were preached in our own vacant parish in Christiansburg, Virginia, only once to as many as a hundred worshipers. Some of these sermons are altogether "new," if there be such a thing, but others have been built on some of my previously preached sermons, which I hope I have improved in the process. Moreover, as you read what I have preached in my elder years, you will notice that I have often become unapologetically autobiographical and occasionally quite personal.

I am writing this book, as you can tell by now, to release something that is buried deep within. More importantly, from the other end of life, I am writing this book to offer inspiration and ideas to younger ministers coming up the slopes behind me. *Pick and choose* from this book what you will, my friends, but make sure you improve it by making it your very own. *Weave*, as you are guided from on high, the themes in this book into the framework of the

11

pericopes our church so helpfully provides. *Borrow* as you find useful the illustrations in these pages and put them into your own words. *Take* the biblical foundations of these messages as the Holy Spirit lifts them up and then run them through your own life and experiences. *Build* these sermons with the help of God into better sermons than I have written here and then preach them as only you can *uniquely* do. *Permit* the thoughts that follow to shine through your own life and experiences and don't hesitate thereby to become autobiographical. You have my permission, my encouragement, and even my blessing to do all this. Then step into your own pulpit to preach the Word of God with *power* and always to the *glory of God.*

Once a young pastor unexpectedly came up to me at a meeting and in the presence of one of my church members, referring to one of my earlier books of published sermons, said, "That was a good book of sermons you published. I have preached them all in my congregation, and I want you to know that my people liked them." That, of course, is plagiarism, though I confess I am human enough to have taken it as a compliment. What I am saying here as clearly as I know how is that you have my permission to take seminal thoughts and themes and illustrations from these written sermons, *only build them into better sermons for your own pulpit ministry.*

Retirement affords one the opportunity to get his or her life into better order and simultaneously tie up some loose ends. These sermons allow one preacher, who has "been down the pike" and "around the block," a chance to come closer to finishing and an attempt to say, at least a few things, *"quite definitely." "For lo! The days are hast'ning on...."*

Some Final Words In Christ's Name!

A Final Sermon Upon the Occasion of Retirement

Elim Lutheran Church
Robbinsdale, Minnesota
October 31, 1993

It is awesome — even scary! — to have been called by the Holy Spirit into the gospel ministry of Word and Sacraments. Many times, not without fear and trembling, I have felt like Jeremiah must have felt when God said to him, "Before I formed you in the womb I knew you, and before you were born I consecrated you; I appointed you a prophet ..." (1:5). My response, sometimes reluctantly, has been that of the prophet Isaiah who said to God that day in the temple, "Here am I; send me!" (6:8). And when it has come to the preaching of the gospel, a frightening responsibility, I have often said as Samuel did *because I needed to*, "Speak, [Lord]; for thy servant heareth" (1 Samuel 3:10 KJV). But for all that, I say to you once again, "If I had a hundred lives to live, I'd be a minister a hundred times."

I had what I consider a good seminary education at Hamma Divinity School. This seminary was located on the beautiful campus of Wittenberg University in Springfield, Ohio. Because of a merger of seminaries, however, Hamma no longer exists and many people in the ELCA have never even heard of it. Moreover, the building in which I learned how to be a pastor has been torn down, and all that remains there is a plot of grass with an inscribed stone marking the place. A year ago at our fortieth seminary class reunion, our class planted a tree on that spot to indicate where our seminary had once stood. Therefore, you might say that I am a clergyman without a seminary.

But I have no ordination papers either. That's right! I cannot find my ordination certificate. I should have framed it and hung it on the wall years ago, but instead I put it away somewhere safe where I knew I could always find it. Now I don't know where it is.

When I came to the Minnesota Synod in 1983 and could not produce this document, Bishop Chilstrom himself had to vouch for my clergy status with the Hennepin County authorities so I might be authorized to officiate at weddings. For the last two months, beginning with the obvious places it might be, I have looked and looked through boxes and files and drawers trying to find this important certificate, but it has eluded me. I trust in retirement when we have more time to look that this precious ordination certificate will somehow show up.

Two weeks after being ordained, I married Mary Fonda Setzer of Louisville, Kentucky. In the beginning of our life together, Mary and I made a deliberate choice. We decided that she would not work outside the home but would devote her full time and talents to homemaking and serving beside me in the ministry. She has been a superb mother to our four children, a fact that is born out by what our children have become. I also want to state publicly, using Paul's words to the Philippians, that I am profoundly "thankful for *her* partnership in the gospel" (RSV). With all my heart I affirm what someone wrote, "During his years in the ministry, Pastor Boye has been assisted, encouraged, and supported by his wife Mary...." And I can enthusiastically affirm what another parishioner said, "You have been blessed by a wife like Mary, and she has been an inspiration to me." Thank you, honey!

In high school when first I seriously considered the ministry, my pastor, the late Reverend Dr. Frederick F. Mueller, talked to me about this calling. One major objection I threw back at him was that I couldn't possibly have enough to say to even get me through the first year in the pulpit. The exact opposite, as he told me, has proved to be the case. I underestimated the enlightenment of the Holy Spirit. One of the exciting challenges, to which I now look forward, is to put together in writing and then hopefully into print some sermons that I never got around to preaching. Even now as the end of my active ministry nears, I have so much left to say that I hardly know where to begin and what to include. More important, I trust today I shall know where to end.

A good starting place, especially on Reformation Sunday, is the Word of God. Luther rediscovered the saving gospel in the Bible and appropriately elevated the Word of God to the position of supreme authority. Here are a couple of texts to gather our thoughts and thereby spring this sermon into action: The Psalmist looked up and said this to God, "Your word is a lamp to my feet and a light to my path." And Saint Paul looked down and wrote this to Timothy, "All scripture is inspired by God and is useful for teaching ..." (2 Timothy 3:16). A primary emphasis of the Lutheran Church, therefore, is that Scripture determines faith and practice. Thus, the Bible is "the sole rule and standard according to which" all doctrines, teachers, and preachers are to be judged. This never meant, however, that Luther was setting up a "paper pope" in the place of the Roman pontiff as a final authority. No! The Reformer's emphasis was on a living, dynamic Word that through the Holy Spirit reaches out to touch our lives relevantly at the points of deepest need. And that is what in my final words from Elim's pulpit I want to talk about this morning. Unable to cover all the ramifications of the centrality of the Bible, I do wish to speak today of two significant ways in which the living, vital, active Word of God is especially relevant to Elim Church.

I

First, God's Word inspires us to respect, love, and deeply appreciate the Church of Jesus Christ! Some may be able to *take the Church for granted,* but I cannot. Some may be able to *trivialize the Church,* but I consider this offensive. Some may be able to say *the Church is irrelevant,* but not I. Some may be able to *wound the Church,* but I believe this is utterly abhorrent. The Bible teaches us reverence for the people of God, the communion of saints, the Church, for, as Ephesians has it, "Christ is the head of the church" (5:23).

Though through the Holy Spirit, the Church came into existence on Pentecost before the completion of the Bible, it is noteworthy that the apostolic Church was deeply rooted and grounded in the Word of God. Before the Bible finally came together, as we know it, with 66 books, at The Council of Carthage in A.D. 397, the early apostles were out preaching the Living Word of the gospel. Dr. T. A. Kantonen, my late seminary professor, said, "The

15

disciples went forth, not with rolls of papyri under their arms but with the Spirit in their hearts and the living gospel on their lips." We know the apostles were familiar with the Old Testament, for time and again in their sermons they quoted the Scriptures they knew so well. Of course, the apostles, too, had their own vivid memories of the life and teachings of Jesus, especially his death on the Cross and his Resurrection from the dead. It wasn't until later, however, that the grand and glorious good news of Christ under the inspiration of the Holy Spirit made its way into writing in what we know as the Gospels and epistles of the New Testament. Along the way these precious documents were copied and recopied and circulated and finally in 397 A.D. brought together into the 66 book canon of the Old and New Testaments as we now know them.

One marvel of that emerging New Testament that never wears out, however, is the way those first Christians *believed* in the Church. They knew it was God's Church, centered in Christ, and brought into being by the Holy Spirit. This reality gave them stability and perspective in those challenging and difficult years when at times it seemed as though the bottom were dropping out. As any student of the Bible knows, the necessary substance of those early epistles, for instance, was correct theology and proper ways to deal with practical church problems. The apostolic Church, you will remember, was often naughty, small, ungrateful, petty, theologically off-center, on a self-destruct course, pounding itself to pieces. With this sort of thing as a backdrop, you would have thought those early Christians would have thrown their hands up in disgust seeing these evils and distortions of truth. You would have thought they would have become weary in having to spend so much time and energy fighting the devil. But they knew the Lord Christ was with the Church, that it was God's own, and that the Holy Spirit would see them through. Those first Christians *really believed* in the Church!

But not only did they really believe in the Church, they also found it to be *indestructible.* That was a miracle, when you think about it, because that small, despised, struggling Christian community was surrounded by the immense, overbearing, and cruel power of the Roman Empire. "Upon this rock," said Jesus to the

16

disciples referring to faith in himself — "upon this rock I will build my church; and the gates of hell shall not prevail against it" (Matthew 16:18). History bears that out, for the historian Will Durant in his book *Christ and Caesar* after 652 pages of history concludes that "There is no greater drama in human record than the sight of a few Christians, scorned or oppressed by a succession of emperors, bearing all trials with a fierce tenacity, multiplying quietly, building order while their enemies generated chaos, fighting the sword with the word, brutality with hope, and at last defeating the strongest state that history has known. *Caesar and Christ had met in the arena, and Christ had won.*" But no wonder! The Church was of God Almighty! We moderns need to remember that and thus be careful neither to hurt the Church nor be ungrateful for it.

But not only is the Church indestructible, it is also *good.* Never mind for now that the present day Church is riddled with problems. Forget for now that some Christians are woeful and pathetic in their Christian witness. Push aside for now the scandals and the divisive and crazy ideas that sometimes plague the Church. What matters is that the Church is good because it is of God. Liz Burns, who became a Christian late in life, wrote in her autobiography, *The Late Liz,*

> *I used to think that the Church was as good or as bad as the people in it. I was wrong. The Church is good, period, and man cannot make it bad no matter how he tries. One can take the purist silk and use it for a dust rag but it remains pure silk. The Church is God's and therefore good and being good, it has survived the use it has been put to, has survived its own clergy, its own members, its ageless persecution. I can damn God but God is not damned. I can belittle His House but His House is not belittled.*

I recently received a letter from a fellow pastor who wrote, "God help us, we mourn for (the Church) sometimes, and sometimes it breaks our hearts, but we love it still, and bow in humility at the thought that simple guys like you and like me have been called by God to ordained ministry in the Church." But wait a minute! At the head of our church bulletin it says, "Ministers: *The People of Elim Church*." As Elimites, I beg of you, treasure the Church, for it is God's own.

II

Second, God's Word became incarnate in and centers around Jesus Christ as Savior and Lord! The Old Testament foreshadowed his coming as God's Anointed, the Messiah. In the fullness of God's time, "The Word became flesh and lived among us" (John 1:14). When the apostles took to preaching, the apostolic message centered in their crucified and risen Lord, and they let it clearly be known that "there is no other name under heaven given among mortals by which we must be saved" (Acts 4:12). Then when you arrive at the last book in the Bible, Revelation, my seminary professor, Dr. Elmer Flack said of it, "No other book makes Christ more central, the Cross more vivid, and Heaven more real." Martin Luther realized the centrality of Jesus Christ in Scripture. He said, "I do not understand anything in Scripture except Christ the Crucified." He said, "Christ is the sum and truth of the Scriptures." He said, "The entire Scripture points only to Christ." He said, "Take Christ out of the Bible and what is left?" And Christ's good word to the Church is this: *"My grace is sufficient for you ..."* (2 Corinthians 12:9).

There is a dramatic scene from the old Martin Luther film of the fifties. Some of his fellow monks with glee brought supposed relics to Martin at the castle church including, so they said, four fragments of Saint Jerome, two fragments of Saint Chrysostom, a veil sprinkled with the blood of the Savior, a nail driven into the Cross, and a fragment of the true Cross. Luther was utterly dismayed at seeing these relics. His father-confessor, John Staupitz, later advised him that the Church can ill afford to tear away the visible support of relics for the common people. "If you leave the Christian to live only by faith with no visible crutches," asked Staupitz, "what will you put in their place?" Luther replied emphatically. "Christ. Man needs *only* Jesus Christ." Let these words sink in here in Elim Church where not infrequently we have gotten off the track: *"Man needs only Jesus Christ."*

Our Lord Christ came into this world bringing salvation. The angel said to Joseph, "... you shall call his name Jesus, for he will save his people from their sins" (RSV). Without Christ the Savior, we are doomed! A few weeks ago a New York executive named Harvey Weinstein was kidnapped and put down in a dark pit underneath the Henry Hudson Parkway. His captors provided very minimal food and shackled his arms and legs so close together that he could not stretch his lanky frame. There for thirteen terrible days he was in a very bad way. Harvey Weinstein found himself fighting against despair until he heard voices calling, "Mr. Weinstein. Mr. Weinstein." He heard his name and hoarsely called back. When his rescuers removed the planks and cinder blocks from the hole, a policeman reached down a hand and lifted him out of that dark pit. That is what God has done for us in Christ! At Christmastide we hear Jesus saying, "From heav'n above to earth I come to bring good news to everyone!"

Today's Second Lesson underscores this grace as Paul exclaimed to the Romans that we "are now justified by his grace as a gift ..." (3:24). Why, people, is it so hard for us to get this matter straight? Why do we keep thinking we have to do something, to contribute something, in order to be saved? Mary Ann Kempcke, whom many of you know, summed up years of experience when she said, "It is amazing the number of Christians that have caught no concept of grace." God accepts us through grace even though we are unacceptable. We are saved by grace alone through faith in Jesus Christ. The Bible says we "are now justified by his grace *as a gift....*" People, we are justified, saved, by his grace alone *as a gift of God.* Now *that* shows how far-reaching is the love of God.

A speaker in seminary, Dr. Ralph Loew, over forty years ago shared this story. Dostoevski, the Russian novelist, tells somewhere of Christ's returning to earth and going to see the pope. The conversation centers around the three temptations. The pope said something like this to the Lord: "Get out of here with those rags. This is how we dress in the Church now. You had your chance to give the whole world bread by just saying the word, and you didn't do it. You could have won the multitudes by simply performing miracles, but you let your chance slip by. You could even have had the whole

19

world in the palm of your hands, but you refused to seize the opportunity when it was right there before you. Because you failed to do these things, we're taking care of everything now. So get out of here, man, with your rags." After this cruel unkindness, so the story runs, Christ walked over to the pope and *kissed him.* God's love in Christ is like that; it will never let us go — no matter how grave the sin.

This question, therefore, leaps out of the Bible and confronts every person: *"What think ye of Christ?"* There is no escaping that question. As you may recall, George Leigh-Mallory, before he set out to scale Mount Everest, was asked, "Why must you climb that awful mountain?" In his classic answer, he said, "Because it is there." There was a fascination about the mountain, an irresistible something he could not ignore; its presence haunted him and he had to do something about it. In fact, he so followed through on that lesser commitment that it cost him his life. How much more is it so with Christ. He is *the* towering figure of history, the grand Galilean, yes, the centerpiece of the Bible. *"What think ye of Christ?"* We have to think something of him. Scripture and life force it upon us. Pilate's question resounds and reverberates through all the centuries, *"What then shall I do with Jesus who is called Christ?"* (Matthew 27:22 RSV). We have to do something with him. We cannot ignore him. We have to somehow respond to him. So why not surrender? Why not fall down and worship him? Why not give your life to him? He is, in Luther's words again, the "sum and truth of the Scriptures." Thus, even now ...

> *Softly and tenderly Jesus is calling,*
> *Calling for you and for me ...*
> *Earnestly, tenderly, Jesus is calling,*
> *Calling, O sinner, come home!*

In the second century there was a frightful martyrdom in the city of Smyrna during the time that a man of some note named Statius Quadratus was the provincial governor or proconsul, as they called such an official in that day. During his time the aged bishop and saint, Polycarp, was brought to trial. The hostile judge pointed

his finger and cried out at the saintly Polycarp who stood innocently before him: "You are to renounce the faith! You are to curse
the name of Christ!" But Polycarp instead gave this inspired answer: "Fourscore and six years have I served him, and he never did
me wrong: how can I revile my King, my Savior?" Outraged, the
government under Statius Quadratus dragged Polycarp to the amphitheater in Smyrna and burned him to death. But the young church
in Smyrna hurled its defiance in the very face of his murderers; for
when later it came to write down in the annals of the church what
had happened, it was very careful to put in the precise date of this
historic event which it noted in this way: "Statius Quadratus, proconsul; *Jesus Christ, King forever!*"

Likewise, "Richard Boye, Senior Pastor of Elim for a while;
JESUS CHRIST, KING FOREVER!" Alleluia! Amen!

The Heart Of The Gospel

A Devotional Meditation at the
Twin Cities College of Senior Clergy

Calvary Lutheran Church,
Golden Valley, Minnesota
November 14, 1995

A dear and godly parishioner once said to me about his Lord, "I am left speechless at his unending love, his generosity, and his grace." Here in these few words is the heart of the gospel: *God's amazing grace!* Soon we will join in singing about this in the first verse of the familiar hymn, "Amazing Grace." All these many years, this is what we have believed in, lived by, and preached on. As the theological center of our Christian faith, God's grace gives us all the courage we need to live our todays and all the confidence we must have to be prepared for our tomorrows. God's mighty reassurance comes to us repeatedly in Scripture in words like these of Paul: "By grace you have been *saved* through faith ..." (Ephesians 2:8) and that is enough.

When I used to read the appointed Gospel on Sundays as an active pastor, I especially liked to land with emphasis on those words in the Lutheran liturgy which come like a powerful exclamation mark at the end of the reading. Those words are these: *The gospel of the Lord!* These five words underscore very significant truth: *The gospel of the Lord! And that gospel is that we are justified by God's grace through faith in Jesus Christ our Savior who died for us and rose again from the dead!* Because our salvation depends entirely on God and not at all on ourselves, we can be *sure of our salvation* and *certain of our eternal destiny.* To illustrate that, I want to share with you from my heart some personal experiences which underscore that which matters most in life — namely, the salvation Jesus came bringing.

My mother died in 1958, and not long afterwards my father, a Danish immigrant, told me he had placed a tombstone on my mother's grave in Kansas City. He also told me he had placed on this tombstone a biblical inscription. When he told me what the verse was, even though it was from the Bible, I did not like it. The verse is this: "My grace is sufficient for you" (2 Corinthians 12:8). Since God's grace is His loving forgiveness and mercy, I imagined people walking by that grave would say to themselves, "My! That woman must have been some sinner, for God's grace is sufficient *even* for her." My mother was a fine Christian woman, and I didn't like that. Dad, however, put me at ease, saying, "Don't worry, son. Nobody can read it. It is inscribed in Danish." So carved on that tombstone are the words of Christ from 2 Corinthians 12, as it has been in our family now for generations: "Min naade er dig nok." "My grace is sufficient for you."

In 1971 we stood at that same grave site stunned, shocked, and deeply saddened to bury my sister who had died by her own hand. I was so traumatized by my sister's untimely death that I cried for weeks even fearing my children would lose respect for me as time and again I collapsed into tears. For many Sundays I could not get through the benediction in church. I would become all choked up and have to step aside as my associate who was primed would then say the benediction in my stead. That April day at the cemetery I looked down at that casket, which never should have been, and then at the inscription wondering if God's grace was sufficient for her. Ironically, she had been active in her church right up to her death and took communion only days previously, but apparently her deepening depression and personal problems overwhelmed her. As we walked away from the grave my father, knowing of both her Christian faith and the severity of her depression, said to me compassionately, "How could God possibly be less merciful than I? Is that not utterly impossible?" I don't want to press that too far, but there is truth in it. God's grace is all-sufficient.

After my mother and sister were gone, my father developed a nagging doubt which, try as I would, I simply could not help him to shake completely. Though a lifelong Lutheran, he longed to have the certainty of salvation which his own father in Denmark had manifested so beautifully on his deathbed. Dad and I had many conversations about this. He turned to me as his son and as a

Lutheran minister. Quite frequently we would get into profound and lengthy discussions on this matter on our walks around the block near our family home in St. Louis. Dad would abruptly stop me on the sidewalk and say, "Little son," — can you imagine him calling me that? — "Little son, how can I *know* I am saved?" I tried to answer that question, *I really did.* I had been to seminary and could quote Scripture, and even though Dad listened respectfully, it did not quite satisfy him. Sometimes I became theological and tried to explain how we can say, "I know I am saved," with no question about it because Christ has promised it and we don't have to save ourselves. We are saved by grace. I told my dear father that if our salvation depended upon perfect goodness with no slips into sin or upon perfect faith with no doubts whatsoever, none of us could ever make it to Heaven. I reminded him that because our salvation depends on Christ alone and not on us, we can therefore be sure and confident of it. We need only in faith accept Jesus Christ as our Lord and Savior. When, despite all this, Dad would still say, "Yes, but, little son, *how can I be sure?*" I would sometimes kiddingly respond, "Well, Dad, even if you were a bank robber or a hit man for the Mafia and you accepted Christ as your Savior, thereby letting the Spirit remake you, you could even then be saved. If the thief on the cross made it into heaven, you surely can!" When all else failed, and it often did, I would end the discussion by smiling at my father and saying, "Well, Dad, someday you will know your little son was right."

My father was a man whose Christian faith reflected itself in his life. Though eighty and six years old, he went to church weekly, took communion regularly, supported the church generously, said his prayers faithfully, and read the Bible daily. When we came to his bedside four hours before he died, the chaplain told us he had already given him the Holy Communion. His own pastor had regularly visited him and prayed with him. An hour before he died, Dad asked me to read from the Bible which I willingly did. Then we prayed together for the last time. Then I said, "Dad, do you believe in Jesus Christ as your Savior and Lord?" He nodded in the affirmative. So he died as he had lived, in the Christian faith. As a symbol of this saving faith, my son whittled a small wooden cross which we placed in his hands and buried with him.

So we came to that Kansas City grave site a third time in 1979, this time to commit my father's earthly body to the ground. After the committal service we graciously asked the people to excuse the family so we could remain privately at the grave for a few moments. Being the last one left in my family of origin, "The Last of the Mohicans," I wanted to see that casket into its final resting place. As the wintery snow was falling that March day, we watched in bitter cold as it was gently put down into the vault. We remained as the vault was sealed. I stood there then for a few moments looking down at that vault with my father's name in raised letters. I thought of the wooden cross he held in his hands, a symbol of salvation. I glanced at the tombstone with its abiding message, "Min naade er dig nok" — *"My grace is sufficient for you."* Then I said in my thoughts, as I am sure he overheard, "Now, Dad, you know your little son was right after all. Now you know salvation is our most certain assurance through the grace of the Lord Jesus Christ." *The gospel of the Lord!*

> *Amazing grace, how sweet the sound,*
> *That saved a wretch like me!*
> *I once was lost, but now am found;*
> *Was blind, but now I see.*

Meditations On Life In Danish Cemeteries

A Sermon Preached in our Son's New Congregation

Peace Lutheran Church
Rogers, Arkansas
November 30, 1997

It is a real privilege to stand here today in this pulpit usually occupied by our son, Erik. Mary and I also wish to express our appreciation for the gracious and generous way in which you have welcomed our son as your pastor as well as his dear wife Deborah and their two precious children Jason and Nathan. Moreover, we want you good people here in Peace Lutheran Church to know that you have been and will continue to be in our prayers.

Last Sunday, Christ the King Sunday, was the last Sunday of the liturgical Church year. Today, the First Sunday in Advent, is the gateway of a new church year. As we find ourselves today straddling two liturgical church years, as it were, this might well be a creative time in a personal way to look back *reflectively* and also to look forward *expectantly*.

But first, you just might like to know what kind of a family background your new pastor has come from. Erik's maternal grandfather, the Reverend Roy B. Setzer, used to take pleasure in kidding me about being a descendent of the Vikings who, as an unfortunate fact of history, were mostly cutthroats and robbers. My father-in-law was so persistent in joking about this that one day I went to my friend, the local butcher, and secured two cow horns. Mary and I then proceeded to make a crude Viking helmet with these horns not unlike that worn by the comic strip character, Hagar the Horrible. I had fun wearing that helmet to dinner one night and just glaring at my dear father-in-law. Actually, this good man had a salutary influence on the whole family as he repeatedly hammered home on us his favorite verse of Scripture: "Seek ye first the kingdom of God" (Matthew 6:33 KJV). Maybe someday Erik will tell you how this charge of Christ, now inscribed on his granddaddy's tombstone, had something to do with his call to the ministry.

My own father was a Danish immigrant who came to this country in April of 1912. Mark that date! Dad came over on a slow and decrepit Danish liner called *Oscar II*. I have seen a picture of that old ship, and it looked as though it could scarcely get out of the Copenhagen harbor. April 1912, however, is quite significant as my father had planned to ferry to England and be aboard the maiden voyage of the *Titanic*. His mother, using her persuasive powers, fortunately talked him out of it, saying, "What's the matter with our good old Danish boats?" Therefore, my father sailed into New York harbor in an old clunker of a ship within a month of when the *Titanic* didn't arrive at all. Along the way you will see that Erik, like his great grandmother, can be quite persuasive.

In this country, my father became a C.P.A. and as such rose to become President of the Missouri State Board of Accountants and a Senior Partner in what only recently because of a merger has become the largest accounting firm in the country. This also might be of some interest to you because one of the former governors of this fair state once publicly called my father a "two-bit schoolboy accountant." He made that statement just before he was run out of office as a result of my dad's audit. This audit and my father's testimony before the Arkansas state legislature clearly showed the errors of that governor's financial ways. Like his paternal grandfather, you will find Erik quite astute and knowledgeable in financial matters.

I happen to be the first pastor to show up in the Boye family, Erik being the second. By way of contrast, there were so many pastors on my wife's side of the family that I used to call it the "holy side of the family" and say that if all these pastors could just agree on anything they could control any synod in the Church. I had planned to become an accountant, a career in which I surely would have failed, when I felt the call to the ministry. Though my dad was somewhat dismayed by this, as a so-called "Happy Dane," he never lost his sense of humor. I'll never forget the day, for example, with a twinkle in his eye he took a tie out of his tie rack and gave it to me. It was a red tie with black sheep on it. As he gave this tie to me he said with a smile, "Son, it is more appropriate that you wear this black sheep tie than I." Guess who has it now?

Far be it from me, however, to suggest that either Erik or I have the distinction of being the blackest sheep in our family. That dubious distinction belongs to one of our ancestors a few generations back named Jens Henrik Boye. When Denmark outlawed capital punishment, he was the last to go. Jens was beheaded for thievery, counterfeiting, and murder before a large crowd of people on August 16, 1856, on the Danish island of Funen. The sword which severed his head from his body is still on display in a Danish museum.

I have tried for years to put a positive spin on this. For one thing, where he was executed near the town of Assens, a hill still bears the name in this present day of "Boye's Hill." Is there anyone here who has had a hill named after them? Furthermore, somewhat like Jesse James, he was such a notorious criminal that at least two biographies have been written on his life. One of these, *Boye and his Gang*, I have in my library at home. I doubt if there is anyone here who has inspired a biography. Before he died, Jens repented of his sins, sincerely apologized to those whom he had wronged, and even turned his considerable talents to writing an inspiring hymn which my cousin has translated for me. Anyone here ever publish a hymn? In the biography in my possession, there are four whole pages just listing the names of the members of Jens Boye's gang. That is roughly equivalent — *roughly equivalent!* — to being the senior pastor of a large congregation like this. Now that your eyelids have become heavy, I will move to more serious matters.

In 1972 my father took Mary and me back to his native Denmark to show us where he had come from. One thing which especially impressed me on that trip was the beauty of Danish cemeteries. Those cemeteries were the most beautiful places in the whole country. They were exquisitely landscaped. Flowers and miniature shrubs were everywhere. The grave sites were lovingly kept and manicured by the surviving families. I'll never forget the day Mary and I sat on a stone bench in a church cemetery on an island in southern Denmark. As we looked out through the trees on to the blue Baltic Sea, I said to my dear wife, "What a place to greet the Lord when he comes again!"

Something other than the beauty, however, arrested my attention even more. It was the symbol of a dove, symbolic of the Holy Spirit, which is so commonplace in those cemeteries. Stone doves were perched on top of many tombstones, and doves were carved into many other tombstones. During those days the Holy Spirit came upon me with a rush as I strolled through those cemeteries and hummed the great hymns of the Church. Surrounded by death, I found myself instead meditating upon life. It is something of this I wish to share with you today.

I

First, I was absolutely fascinated by the names inscribed on the tombstones. Some of those names are not common here in the United States, such as Ivar, Viggo, Aage, Emil, Rasmus, and Bengt. Some of the names are similar to but still different from what we name our own children such as Peder, Poul, Birthe, Johanne, and Henrik. But some of the names are identical to ones used here such as Karen, Carl, Julie, Alfred, Marie, and Ellen. At this the Holy Spirit prompted me to consider how easily we fall into the trap of stressing our differences as human beings when what we ought to do is to reach out to find common ground. My friends, we're all cut from the same human cloth. We all have the same emotions, the same frailties, and even much the same problems. We are all stained by the same original sin. Why, therefore, can't we be more respectful and understanding of other people? Rodney King kind of stumbled into putting this rather well when he said, "Can't we all just get along?"

Certainly that is applicable to the divisiveness we so often see here in the United States. Patrick Henry gave a speech before the first Colonial Congress in 1774. He said, "Throughout the continent government is dissolved. Landmarks are dissolved. Where are now your boundaries? The distinctions between Virginians, Pennsylvanians, New Yorkers, New Englanders are no more. I am not a Virginian, I am an American." An historian wrote, "Forty-three delegates sat spellbound, hypnotized altogether. It was crazy what they had just heard: they knew it was crazy; an American, in God's name what was that?" But the future was with that unity! Ought we not, therefore, as citizens of this great land focus on the things which unite us rather than those things which divide us?

Even more important, should we not as Christians recognize our oneness in Christ Jesus? Our Lord himself prayed "that [we] may all be one" (John 17:11). And Paul wrote to the Galatians, "There is no longer Jew or Greek, there is no longer slave or free, there is no longer male and female; for all of you are one in Christ Jesus" (3:28). And we even sing, "We are one in the Spirit, we are one in the Lord...." How then can any Christian pretend to be superior to another? How then can any Christian group arrogantly claim to have the whole truth to the exclusion of all others? How then can there sometimes be congregational squabbles? How then can families who call themselves Christians sometimes be so tragically divided? *Are we not all "Children of the Heavenly Father"?* Even as the Holy Spirit caused me to be fascinated by the names on those tombstones, I learned to look respectfully for commonality, not differences, in other human beings.

II

Second, I was forcibly struck by the many evidences of Christianity in those cemeteries. Crosses, doves, Bible verses, open Bibles, and other Christian symbols were carved into nearly every tombstone. Were a man from Mars to visit those cemeteries, he would surely think those people were most certainly Christians.

I was perplexed, however, because what I saw in those cemeteries was so incongruent with what I saw elsewhere in Denmark. To paraphrase Isaiah, "This people honors me with their [tombstones] but their hearts are far from me." *There is, for instance, pathetic churchgoing in the Church of Denmark.* Mary and I with our folks worshiped one Sunday at the famous Grundvig Cathedral in Copenhagen. Though this church seats 2,000, there were only 47 of us at church that day at the one and only service. *Again, there is rampant pornography everywhere in that country.* Suffice it to say that you would be shocked in seeing blatant pornographic magazines so prominently displayed in drugstore windows and

31

elsewhere. *Still again, there is superficial Christianity reflected in the government.* My cousin told me that the Danish government had outrageously fired two pastors because, obeying God rather than man, these two godly men had refused to do what the government wrongly demanded. As I walked through those cemeteries I couldn't help but think of those hard, biting words of the Lord in Revelation. "I know your works," said Jesus to the church at Laodicea, "you are neither cold nor hot. I wish that you were either cold or hot. So, because you are lukewarm, and neither cold nor hot, I am about to spit you out of my mouth."

But wait! Jesus *also* said, "Judge not, that you be not judged" (Matthew 7:1 RSV). My friends, what about *our* Christianity? Certainly Christianity is more than symbolism in a cemetery, but how deep does it go in our own lives? I was an active Lutheran minister for more than 41 years, and I want you to know that I saw more than I care to remember of church members *trivializing* Christianity. To be sure, we readily profess to be Christians, do we not, but how many are there among us who talk the talk but do not walk the walk, whose priorities are topsy-turvy, whose word and integrity cannot be trusted, who are quick to "see the speck in [another person's] eye, but do not notice the log in [their] own eye," (Matthew 7:3) who play fast and loose with their commitment to the church, and above all, who are lukewarm in their relationship to Jesus Christ as Savior and Lord? Need I say more? I was indeed struck then by those many evidences of Christianity in Danish cemeteries, but I am far more impressed now by those who take their faith seriously. I beg of you to take that thought home today, as I did, and spiritually chew on it with the help of the Spirit of God.

III

Third, I was hugely uplifted by a common inscription: Tak for alt. As you can easily guess, that frequently used Danish expression means: Thanks for everything. I am telling you these words, Tak for alt, are inscribed all over Danish cemeteries. They seemed to reflect a profound attitude of gratitude. Only recently having observed Thanksgiving Day, we ought to have this attitude in the forefront of our minds. Moreover, Karl Barth, the great theologian, has pointedly reminded us that "basically and radically all sin is ingratitude." Therefore, a critical thing in life is *always* whether we take things for granted or with gratitude.

Those nine lepers sadly took Jesus' healing for granted, but in my years in the ministry, by way of contrast, I thank God for the inspiring examples I have seen in those who have accepted life with gratitude even in unlikely circumstances. In my second parish, for instance, a sorely tested woman wrote to me, "I am thankful. I love God who never lets me down. I am thankful that I can be thankful with all my heartaches." *"I am thankful that I can be thankful with all my heartaches."* Is that not a magnificent Christian attitude? In another of my parishes a middle-aged man dying of cancer said to me only days before he died, "I really lived quite a life, and I'm thankful for what I have." *"I am thankful for what I have."* Is that not a splendid Christian spirit? And only recently a friend and former church councilman wrote to me concerning his own health problems and the deteriorating physical condition of his wife who is almost certainly terminal. Then he wrote this sentence: "We continue to rejoice in the Lord for his faithfulness, blessings, and hope of the future." *"We continue to rejoice in the Lord...."* Is that not an awesome Christian perspective? Truly grateful people, you see, can celebrate God's goodness *even* amid the pains of life because above all *they know God is with them.* As it was foretold, "... his name shall be called Emmanuel (which means, God with us)" (RSV).

Therefore this first Sunday of a new church year let us recapture the authentic thrill of the Advent season; let us take with deep gratitude and *not* for granted that "... when the fullness of time had come, God sent His Son..." and "... the Word became flesh and dwelt among us" (RSV). Would that this day we could all feel down into the marrow of our souls the excitement of the glory of the coming of the Lord! Would that this day we could all go out from this place determined to live out gratefully our faith in response to "the grace of the Lord Jesus Christ" and "the love of God" and "the communion of the Holy Spirit." A quarter of a century ago, *under the influence of the Spirit of Christ*, I pondered long and hard the meaning of those Danish words, which have become so dear to

33

me, Tak for alt. And I prayed, "Thanks, Lord, for everything!" And I exclaimed, "Thanks be to God for His inexpressible gift!" (RSV).

In this blessed Advent season let us truly prepare ourselves for Christmas when we humbly bow down our lives to worship the Christ Child, the "babe wrapped in swaddling clothes, lying in a manger" (KJV). Let us also prepare ourselves for the Second Coming of the Lord, for in the words of the Creed, "He will come again to judge the living and the dead."

There is a wonderful old hymn, which I hummed as I strolled through those Danish cemeteries. It is a hymn which was included in the old *Common Service Book* but which somehow didn't make it into either the red *Service Book and Hymnal* or the green *Lutheran Book of Worship*. I want to end today by quoting the first verse of that hymn which brings together what we have been saying here this morning. Listen:

> *A few more years shall roll,*
> *A few more seasons come,*
> *And we shall be with those that rest*
> *Asleep within the tomb.*
> *Then, O my Lord, prepare*
> *My soul for that great day;*
> *O wash me in Thy precious Blood,*
> *And take my sins away.*

"O wash me in Thy precious Blood, And take my sins away." Amen!

34

Justification By Grace Through Faith

A Sermon Preached on the Occasion of
1917 — The Diamond Jubilee — 1992

Good Shepherd Lutheran Church
Southampton, Pennsylvania
October 25, 1992

Every one of us at one time or another, has asked the question put by the Philippian jailer: "What must I do to be saved?" (Acts 16:30). The *correct* answer is: "Believe on the Lord Jesus, and you will be saved ..." (Acts 16:31). Here in a nutshell is the doctrine of justification by grace through faith.

The right of Christianity to exist rests on the proclamation of this doctrine. It is the chief article of the gospel. Justification by grace through faith is the truth that makes Christianity *Christian* and the Church really *the Church.* Its acceptance by the individual Christian is essential for salvation. The preferred way of stating this doctrine is, as my title indicates, justification by grace through faith. This makes it clear that salvation is more than a matter of believing hard enough; it is a matter of humbly receiving what God has done through faith.

The authority for this doctrine is the Bible. Scripture teaches justification by grace through faith from beginning to end. Already in the fifteenth chapter of Genesis we read that Abraham "believed the LORD; and the LORD reckoned it to him as righteousness." Abraham's faith in God's sight made him righteous, that is, acceptable to God. Saint Paul quoted this many centuries later in Romans and again in Galatians. Like the theme of a great symphony repeated over and over this doctrine of justification by grace through faith sounds all the way through the Bible. Hear it now as recorded in our Second Lesson for Reformation Sunday from Romans 3:23: "... since all have sinned and fall short of the glory of God; they are now justified by his grace as a gift, through

35

the redemption that is in Christ Jesus ... For we hold that a person is justified by faith apart from works prescribed by the law."

Luther, you will remember, tried to storm heaven by being a moral rigorist and a monastic athlete. This brought him only torment of soul. He realized he could never do enough to become righteous in the sight of a holy God. Then through his earnest study of the Bible, the scriptural truth of justification by grace through faith leapt in upon him in such an overwhelming way that he felt the very gates of heaven had been opened to him. Furthermore, it was his steadfast insistence on this doctrine that led him to that historic confrontation at the Diet of Worms where he so boldly planted his feet and so courageously said, "Here I stand!" Luther vividly rediscovered a great scriptural reality that had been embedded in the Bible all the while — namely, that by grace we are saved through faith as a gift of God and not of ourselves. Do see now how this crucial doctrine works out for our salvation.

I

To begin with, this doctrine takes *sin* seriously! Luther said the problem is not sins but sin. Anyone thinking of the seven deadly sins and the Ten Commandments can come up with many individual sins, but sin itself is something far worse, far deeper than that. Moreover, we are all afflicted by sin. Sin is a broken relationship with God, a rebellion against what God wants for us, a lack of trust in God. Sin is a turning inward toward ourselves rather than upward toward God and outward toward other people. Sin is an arrogant sense of self-sufficiency.

The Scripture is blunt about our human predicament. Psalm 143:2: "... no one living is righteous before (God)." Romans 3:10: "There is no one who is righteous, not even one." And again in Romans, "All have sinned and fall short of the glory of God" (3:23). In today's Gospel from John 8:34, Jesus said, "Everyone who commits sin is a slave to sin," and to the man who put his trust in worldly goods rather than God, the Master himself said, "You fool! This very night your life is being demanded of you" (Luke 12:20). So serious is our human plight that the hymn writer cried out from the depths of his soul, "Lord Jesus, think on me and purge away my sin."

Sin inevitably shows up in a life that leaves little or no room for God. A writer, for instance, with topsy-turvy priorities said, "The first right on earth is the right of the ego." A sports broadcaster proudly commented, "I really believe I'm the best. My relationship with the men who play the games — all games — is probably unparalleled in this country." A politician's wife of a former campaign had the audacity to say this: "I have talent. I know I'm smart. I got straight A's in graduate school. I've still got my looks. I've got all these terrific things going for me. I mean, my (gracious) you are talking to, I think, one of the most fascinating women in this country." A business leader arrogantly looking back on his record: "I got pretty (darn) good." An athlete speaking of his exploits: "It ain't no accident that I'm the greatest man in the world at this time of history." Where in such attitudes is there room for God? And that is what sin is, denying God kingship in our lives and enthroning ourselves. That's serious — salvation-threatening! — and face it: none of us has will power enough to rid ourselves of that tendency.

II

Therefore, this doctrine takes the *cross* seriously! God had to do something drastic to remedy the serious problem of sin. He had to take the initiative and act in order to alter the situation of the sinner. He had to make the unrighteous, *righteous*. He therefore sent His Son into the world to die on Calvary's Cross. Our Lord Christ came to save the world, and this was God's way, to die on a cruel Cross in our place, taking our sins upon himself. It took that much to win salvation for us. In this apparent tragedy, a divine purpose was at work. The Cross is not God's defeat but God's victory in our behalf. Christ paid the price for our sins thereby opening up the way to God. Because of Christ's sacrificial death on Calvary, God declares us "not guilty!" He pronounces us righteous. He justifies us even though we be ungodly.

You don't need to take this from me, but if you want to be saved, you had better take it from the Bible. Romans 5:6: "For while we were still weak, at the right time Christ died for the ungodly." John 3:17: "God did not send the Son into the world to condemn the world, but in order that the world might be saved through him." Acts 4:12: "There is salvation in no one else, for there is no other name under heaven given among mortals by which we must be saved." Or, perhaps it was put most simply in the words of the hymnist: "Just as I am, without one plea, but that thy blood was shed for me."

There is an old story of a little boy who made a boat and took it with him to the river to play. It happened the boat drifted out of the shallow waters and into the stream where it was soon carried far beyond his reach. Time passed. Then one day the little boy saw his own boat on display in a store window. Of course, he hurried into the store to see how he could recover it. The storekeeper explained that the only way he could get the boat back was to pay the price which was marked on it. Out of his little pocket came his treasures, and the small boy counted his coins. But it was not enough. Home he ran to his father to get the additional money; then back to the store. How his little heart rejoiced as he paid the price and reclaimed his own boat. As he walked out of the store, the little fellow was heard to say, "Now little boat, you are twice mine — you are mine because I made you and mine because I bought you!" God does something like that for us. He created us and we strayed. Then He bought us back again with the blood of His own son on the Cross. So serious is our plight that Jesus went as far as even God could go, saying, "This is my body ... broken *for you*" (1 Corinthians 11:24 KJV).

III

It follows that this doctrine takes *faith* seriously! This important doctrine does not depend on being understood; it depends on being *received*. And it is faith which receives God's gift of His unmerited grace and forgiveness. What can a man or woman do to merit salvation? Nothing! All you or I can do is to let God's glorious gift of salvation flow into our lives through faith. In the words of Stewart of Edinburgh — "For me, Paul would say religion began on the day when I ceased straining and striving and struggling for heaven's favor, and was content to bow my head and accept the

38

gift I could never win." Salvation is God's gift; all we can do is receive it through faith.

Listen to our text from Romans 3 again, this time from the Revised Standard Version: "They are justified by his grace as a gift, through the redemption which is in Christ Jesus ... to be received by faith" Did you get that? "... to be *received by faith*." Perhaps it has been most simply put by the hymn writer who has caused us to sing "My faith looks up to thee, thou Lamb of Calvary, Savior divine!"

Some of you will remember Ray Norton, a former member of Good Shepherd, who is now deceased. He was a highly successful automobile dealer in Philadelphia. One night some years ago, when we were guests in his home for dinner, Ray pulled a bill from his wallet to show to me telling me he had concluded some big car transaction. I had never seen a bill like that before. It had a picture on it of someone unfamiliar to me, not any President I could remember. The picture fascinated me. It was a picture of a man named Salmon P. Chase who, I later learned, was the founder of the Federal Reserve System. But then, my eyes just about jumped out of my head when I saw I was actually holding a $10,000 bill. Well, suppose I had a $10,000 bill here this morning and wanted to give it away. It could make you rich. I could walk up and down the aisle of the church offering it to anyone who would take it. But what good would that do if you wouldn't receive it? You could protest to me, "You aren't really willing to give away that much money, are you?" You could say, "I earn my money and will not take anything for nothing." You could claim, "It's just too good to be true." But, my friends, God is already willing to give us something of exceedingly more value than any $10,000 bill. He is willing to give us eternal salvation with a guarantee of the Kingdom of Heaven. *But we have to take it! We have to believe God wants to give it! We have to humbly accept His inestimable gift of salvation through faith!*

IV

As a final consequence of what has been said, this doctrine takes *new life* seriously! I hope along the way you have noted the progression of what we are saying this morning. The doctrine of justification by grace through faith, you see, takes *sin* seriously, it takes the *Cross* seriously, it takes *faith* seriously, and now we are concluding with the inevitable consequence that this doctrine takes *new life* seriously. It is not true that good works are necessary for salvation; what is true is that salvation is necessary for good works. As Luther put it, "Faith is a divine work which changes us and births us anew out of God." Thereby authentic Christian goodness becomes a matter of *thanksgiving*. When we are able to stop striving for Heaven, then we can relax, as it were, and look around to notice the needs of our neighbor and thank God by serving him. When the ego gets out of the way, we are able to just go about doing good and being good to give praise to God. When the "have to" ceases being our motivation, there is room for the "want to" to move in and take over and give God the credit. When self is dethroned in our hearts, then Christ himself becomes our King of kings and Lord of lords whom we worship and adore. Moreover, authentic Christian goodness becomes a matter of *inwardness*. We might compare this to a musician. To be a musician of quality, you must, of course, know something of the technique of music. You must familiarize yourself with such things as scales, tones, flats, measures, and harmonies. But to really be a musician, *you must have music in you.* It isn't enough to know all the rules about music, you must have music *in you.* So also to live the Christian life, you must have Christ himself *in you.*

Consider a couple of verses from the New Testament. Paul wrote to the Romans that "... we have been buried with him by baptism into death, so that, just as Christ was raised from the dead by the glory of the Father, so we too might walk in *newness of life*" (6:4). Again to the Corinthians, the great apostle wrote, "If anyone is in Christ, there is a *new creation*" (2 Corinthians 5:17 RSV). As the hymnist expressed it, "I give thee back the life I owe, that in thine ocean depths its flow, may richer, fuller be."

In 1989 I took a memorable automobile trip from Nashville, Tennessee, to Bozeman, Montana, with a dear son-in-law, our daughter Kirsten's husband Rhett. Along the way we stopped in St. Louis where, among other things, we visited the old Union Station. When I was in high school during the war years, we often

40

went down there to meet my dad returning from business trips. Later I took many train trips in and out of that station going to college and seminary. I remember that railroad station in its heyday when it was busy, impressive, and exciting. Then in the 1950s and the 1960s and into the 1970s that railroad station deteriorated badly, as train travel lessened, until it became an ugly, dilapidated eyesore, an embarrassment to the city of St. Louis. Many people wanted to tear it down and get rid of it. Instead, however, a developer totally renovated it, until what is seen there now, for those who remember how bad it was, is amazing. *Time* magazine even had an article on it. This former railroad station has become a city within a city, bright, beautiful, functional. It is said that if you had enough money, you could live there and never leave. There is a large shopping mall, a hotel, an open domed park with fountains, ponds, and gardens, and plenty of places to eat. I have never with these eyes seen such an impressive restoration. From the outside, that Union Station looks pretty much as it always did, except it has been cleaned up, but the inside is totally different. If ever you visit St. Louis, this old station is the number one place, even before the Arch, you ought to visit. Only a few years ago, it was a rotting eyesore, dusty and dark, with the paint peeling off, the kind of place you wouldn't want to visit. But now it is totally new! And it is good for something too! So also is new life in Christ.

God's "amazing grace" streaming down from Calvary wipes away our sin as though it had never been. When we thus receive His gift of salvation through faith, we are made over into new creations. This is the gospel of the Lord!

Keep Your Eyes On The Sign

A Seventy-Fifth Anniversary Sermon

Elim Lutheran Church
Robbinsdale, Minnesota
March 9, 1997

Grace and peace to you from God our Father and our Lord Jesus Christ. Amen.

As recorded in today's Gospel, Jesus said, "... as Moses lifted up the serpent in the wilderness, so must the Son of Man be lifted up, that whoever believes in Him may have eternal life. For God so loved the world that He gave His only Son, so that everyone who believes in him may not perish but may have eternal life" (John 3:14-16).

I want to thank Pastor Floe and the seventy-fifth Anniversary Committee for their kind and gracious invitation to be here today and to have the privilege once again of standing in this pulpit. It is also good to look out across this worshiping congregation and see the familiar faces of our Elim friends. I have missed you in my retirement years though I have often had occasion to think about you as I would drive by this church and as I would see some of you from time to time in our community. You have been and will always be in my prayers. What I feel very deeply this morning is well expressed in the beginning words of an old Transfiguration hymn: "'Tis good, Lord, to be here!"

Furthermore, I salute your committee for the selection of a theme for this anniversary year. A more appropriate theme for a seventy-fifth anniversary than *Lift High The Cross* could not have been chosen. This was the emphasis of my own ministry which spanned more than four decades during which time I was privileged to serve in five fine congregations. As you may recall, I closed my ministry here by singing with you in the recessional the same hymn with which we began today, the title of which serves so well as your anniversary theme.

Appropriately in this church the Cross *is* high and lifted up. In our Gospel Jesus said, "... as Moses lifted up the serpent in the wilderness, so must the Son of Man be lifted up." Elsewhere Jesus said, "And I, when I am lifted up from the earth, will draw all people to myself." The uplifted Cross focuses on our Lord and Savior, Jesus Christ, and points straightaway to the preeminent doctrine of Christianity — namely, justification by grace alone through faith. As Saint Paul put it in today's Second Lesson, "For by grace you have been saved through faith, and this is not your own doing; it is the gift of God." We are free to reject this heavenly gift, of course, and we are free to rebel against God's will, if we choose, but it is to our own detriment. The Cross of Christ makes absolutely central God's grace which Lowell Erdahl defines as "the undeserved mercy and life-giving power that welcomes us as we are and empowers us to become what we can be." That is to say, we do not need to stay the way we are. Thus, *Lift High The Cross* is a most appropriate and insightful gospel theme for a seventy-fifth anniversary year.

Still, in our earth-bound humanness, we can never fully fathom the profundity of the Cross. As an old man, whose days were numbered, said as he gazed out on the boundless ocean, "The sea always grows greater." So also the Cross of Christ "tow'ring o'er the wrecks of time" grows ever greater. We can be sure that God's love streams down from that uplifted Cross. We can be sure, too, that the power of God's love epitomized in *the old rugged Cross* is a power which reaches into our daily lives. And that is what I want to talk about with you this morning, the power of the Cross for daily living.

I

I would ask you to notice first, therefore, that the love of God streaming down from the Cross is more than enough to **save any and all of us from our sins**. No one need be excluded. No, not one! The Cross symbolizes the divine love which is readily available to save anyone. We need that, don't we? Who here has had all the badness drained out of them? Who here has not done wicked enough things to cause God displeasure? Who here is able to throw the first stone at someone for being mean and harboring mean thoughts? Who here has accumulated enough good works to assault God's throne demanding to be saved? None of us, that's who! My friends, the deepest, most fundamental need of humankind is to be saved from sin.

It is crucial, therefore, that we receive forgiveness from God. Thus, on Calvary God did for us what we cannot do for ourselves. "He died that we might be forgiv'n." Caiaphas, who didn't mean to do it, nevertheless, inadvertently stumbled on to a profound truth when he blurted out, "It [is] expedient ... that one man should die for the people." Though Scripture is saturated with evidences of God's love, so often humankind just didn't get it. To break through to us it took that one crowning day of history when "Love divine, all loves excelling" leapt out at us through Christ who climbed Calvary and died there for our sins. That crumpled our defenses and broke through to us as nothing else could. Thank God! "He died that we might be forgiv'n."

But that old Lenten hymn continues, "He died to make us good." In gratitude to God for being saved, we willingly repent of our sins and seek to live lives more consistent with His will. Here again we are not alone. God sent us the Holy Spirit to bring renewal and to boost all our efforts to do the right. Thus Paul could write, "... if anyone is in Christ, there is a new creation" (2 Corinthians 5:17). This is how far God's love goes both to save us from our sins as well as to rescue us from our human tendencies toward self-destruction. Thus as we *Lift High the Cross* we remember the truth so well expressed by the hymnist that "... the love of God is broader than the measure of our mind."

Some years ago I invited a young professor from Eastern Baptist College in Philadelphia to preach a couple of times at the church I was serving in that area. His two sermons were so compelling that we could never forget this man. His name was Tony Campolo. Since then he has become quite famous as an evangelist and also as a spirtual adviser to President Clinton. Recently I read something interesting about him in Jimmy Carter's fine book, *Living Faith*. President Carter tells about Tony visiting an all-night diner in Hawaii when he was suffering from jet lag and unable to sleep. From his booth he happened to hear several "ladies of the night" talking. One of them told the others that she was going to be 39 years old the next day and that in her whole lifetime she had never had a birthday party. Well, it was just like the Tony Campolo I know to arrange with the manager at his expense to throw a surprise party the next night for this woman and her friends. When they came together the next night after plying their immoral trade, they were stunned and thrilled to find this surprise party waiting for them. After treating these "ladies of the night" to this party, he visited with them, doubtless bringing them cheer with his terrific sense of humor even as he witnessed to them. Tony then led these ladies in a word of prayer. Can you imagine that? Later the diner manager asked him, "What kind of a church do you belong to?" Tony shot right back, "I belong to the kind of church that throws birthday parties for [prostitutes] at 3:30 in the morning." *The love of God is broader than the measure of our mind!*

Jimmy Carter then wrote, "This was Jesus' kind of Church." Jesus' kind of Church is one where *everybody* is touched by God's love, where *nobody* however bad is excluded, and where *anybody* can be gifted with new life. Love like that radiates out from the Cross of Christ. As long as I live, my friends, I will continue to pray that Elim will ever stay the course by being that kind of spiritually welcoming church which lifts up high the Cross of Jesus Christ. God's only Son died on that Cross "so that everyone" — hear that! — "*everyone* who believes in him may not perish ..." (John 3:16).

II

I would ask you to notice second, now, that the love of God streaming down from the Cross is more than enough to **secure us for time and eternity**. First God's love on the Cross *saves* us from sin; then it *secures* us for eternal life. Faith in Jesus Christ as our personal Lord and Savior is the *guarantee* of the Kingdom of Heaven.

Do not think me so insensitive that after being away for three and a half years I do not notice that some familiar faces and faithful members are no longer here. As the old funeral liturgy has it, "In the midst of life we are in death." That simply is the way it is. Death comes to us all in time, sometimes prematurely, but even before that it strikes our loved ones and moves us to tears. God knows how many tears have been shed in this very place at funerals.

But lift up your eyes, my friends, above where the casket of your loved one was once placed. Look up and see the *empty* Cross. Christ is no longer hanging there. Though we confess in the Creed that " ... he was crucified, died, and was buried," we go on to state that "on the third day he rose again." When the New Testament writers speak of the Cross, they always see it in the light of the Easter glory. The crucifixion and the resurrection cannot be separated. The resurrection is the exclamation mark, as it were, at the end of God's eternal plan of salvation. It is God's signature of love at the end of a plan for saving us in this world and for the world to come.

Everything that had been building in Scripture came to a resounding crescendo on that "first day of the week, while it was still dark" when the women at the tomb were astounded as an angel shattered their grief asunder, saying of the crucified Christ, "He has risen, he is not here; see the place where they laid him" (RSV). This is fundamental in our Christian Faith. Paul was right when he wrote, "If Christ has not been raised, your faith is futile ... But in fact," Paul continued, "Christ *has been raised* from the dead!" (1 Corinthians 15:17, 20). Again and again, for us Christians that kind of faith surfaces and empowers us in our daily lives.

A year or so ago I was in the airport to meet one of my children, and while there I happened to recognize and walk right by one of my spiritual heroes, Chicago's Cardinal Joseph Bernardin. I continued walking down the concourse, but then I turned around and walked back, saying to myself that I wanted to meet that man, if I could, and shake his hand. I walked up and stood nearby waiting to see if the Cardinal would come over and speak to me. In a minute or so he ever so graciously walked over to me, shook my hand, and gave me a chance to introduce myself. We then talked together for a few minutes. As we conversed and spoke of a mutual pastor friend, I felt I was in the presence of spiritual greatness. I knew then Cardinal Bernardin had been sick, and, as you know, he has since died. Before he died, however, he wrote a book titled *The Gift of Peace*, in which he said, "As one who is dying, I have especially come to appreciate the gift of life." It is true: *In the midst of life we are in death!* Furthermore, before this saintly man died he made this memorable statement: "We can look at death in two ways, as an enemy or as a friend. As a person of faith, I see death as a friend." Without the resurrection, no one can say that.

Men like the Cardinal teach us something about both life and death. I shall continue to pray, therefore, that Elim will go right on out into the future lifting high the empty Cross of Christ and proclaiming the power of the Resurrection. According to our text underscoring God's love, not only do we "not perish" because of our sins but also and *especially* we have "eternal life" because Christ rose from the dead.

See now where this lands us! *Lift high the Cross, the love of God proclaim* — this, my friends, is what churches are for. This is our mission to the world which we dare not abandon. Still, at our own spiritual peril, we as individuals or as congregations sadly can become *distracted* and *off-center* and *lose our focus* on the Cross of Christ. We can thus *lose our way* and consequently *forfeit our souls* even *as the Spirit departs from us* and *the darkness engulfs us.* Spiritually, we can so easily become lost in the night.

I want to illustrate this spiritual lostness, its cause and cure, with something which may initially seem irrelevant but stay with me. I want to share with you some things about, of all things, the Verrazano-Narrows Bridge in New York City. This great bridge, named after an Italian explorer, crosses from Staten Island to Brooklyn. It stands like a colossus astride the entrance to the New York harbor. The seventy story twin towers, which hold the bridge up so that it will never fall down, are firmly built on solid rock. These towers are so high and so far apart that, because of the curvature of the earth, they are 1.625 inches farther apart at the top than they are at the bottom. I'm sure you have seen pictures of this magnificent bridge as it is the one where on television every year we see thousands and thousands of runners cross to begin the New York City Marathon.

Awesome and beautiful as this eye-catching bridge is, however, *it is not enough to just look at it.* Structurally sound and strategically located as this bridge is, *that in itself will never get you over into Brooklyn and on out to Long Island.* No, you must *pay attention* to what you are doing, or you will be in trouble.

Last October Mary and I drove across this Verrazano-Narrows Bridge, which we had done many times before while living in the East, but this time I became distracted by trying to catch a glimpse of the Statue of Liberty and the New York skyline. Because I did not concentrate on where we were going, we got lost. First, I accidentally missed a turn and we drove on to the lower level where the trucks go rather than the more familiar upper level where the cars generally go. Then at the other end of the bridge I missed the sign for the Southern Parkway which goes out on to Long Island where we wanted to go. Furthermore, I became confused, forgetting that to go east on the Southern Parkway you must first wind around in the opposite direction. After a series of turns trying to recover from my mistakes, we ended up lost on the unsafe streets of Brooklyn at night. Let me tell you, good people, that was scary!

As we continued to drive around I became so disoriented, I did not even know which direction it was back to the bridge. Moreover, on the dimly lit streets of Brooklyn and without a flashlight, we could not see the street signs which made our map useless. I would like very much to blame this predicament on my wife, but that wouldn't be fair. The problem in crossing this bridge, awesome as it is to behold and functional as it is in facilitating traffic — the problem is that you still have to watch what you are doing. And, though I am not one of those men who is reluctant to stop and ask for directions, I want you to know that I was too terrified on the crime-ridden streets of Brooklyn to get out of my well-packed, safely-locked car with a Minnesota license to ask anybody where I was. Believe me, it is a most frightening experience as a stranger to be lost in Brooklyn in the dark of night. We felt like robbery-vulnerable morgue-bait.

Suddenly we came on a big fire. I never thought I would be glad to see a building burning down, but it was comforting to come on a policeman there directing traffic. I stopped the traffic with my car and asked that policeman out of the window how I could possibly pick up the Southern Parkway. He quickly ascertained that we were strangers in trouble whereupon he directed us down the wrong way on a one way street. I said, "But officer, that is a one way street!" Sensing, I think, both my fear as well as the potential danger, he pointed his finger and said something like this to me, and he said it *very emphatically*, "Go down that street *anyway*. Turn left at Second Avenue, and look for signs to the Parkway at Sixty-seventh Street!" He did what faithful pastors do: he pointed *the way*!

We followed his directions, halfway expecting someone to shoot us in the process, but fortunately all we got were some dirty New York looks. By then carefully watching the signs on a better lighted main thoroughfare we finally got safely back on to the right road which took us to our destination which was the city of Riverhead on Long Island. This famous bridge, you see, so splendid to look at, so superior to the Brooklyn ferry it replaced, and so spectacular to look out from — this bridge does not automatically take someone to the right place. No! It is required that you must *stay focused on what you are doing and where you are going*! Lest you go astray, *you must keep your eyes on the signs*!

The Cross, too, is a sign, a sign of *incomparable significance*! It is therefore imperative that we keep focused on it as a symbol of salvation and eternity. So, *keep your eyes on the sign*: it will draw you closer to the One who said, "I am the way!" *Keep your eyes on the sign*: if you become distracted, the Spirit may depart from you and you may become lost in the night. *Keep your eyes on the sign of the Cross*: All God's promises come together in this symbol. *Lift High the Cross!* It is *the* sign, *the* symbol, that embodies "the power of God for salvation to everyone who has faith ..." And while you're at it, don't build your lives on sinking sand either. Build your lives firmly *On Christ, the solid Rock*. For "everyone who believes in [Christ will] not perish but ... have eternal life." May God so bless you now and always. Amen!

Reflections On A Prayer For All Seasons

A Sermon for the One Hundred and Fortieth Anniversary Year

Good Shepherd Lutheran Church
(Formerly Amity Lutheran Church)
Lena, Illinois
May 11, 1997

Let us pray:

> *Lord God, you have called your servants to ventures of*
> *which we cannot see the ending, by paths as yet*
> *untrodden, through perils unknown. Give us faith to go*
> *out with good courage, not knowing where we go, but*
> *only that your hand is leading us and your love sup-*
> *porting us; through Jesus Christ our Lord. Amen.*[1]

Last Thursday was the Day of Ascension, when, according to
Acts 1:8, Jesus said to the apostles, "... you will be my witnesses in
Jerusalem, in all Judea and Samaria, and to the ends of the earth."
Though they knew Jerusalem, where their Lord had been crucified, and though they knew Judea and Samaria, where the Master
had taught and healed, they did not know where the ends of the
earth might be. On the Day of Ascension, Jesus also said, "... you
will receive power when the Holy Spirit has come upon you" (Acts
1:8). Ten days later on the Day of Pentecost, according to Acts 2:4,
"All of them were filled with the Holy Spirit." Though they had
hardly a clue as to what might lie ahead, they had an enormous
resource upon which to count, as they would find out: they would
have the Holy Spirit. The Spirit of Christ was to meet their uncer-
tainty with guidance and their weakness with power thus enabling
them to face the future with *boldness.*

My friends, we, too, as servants of the Most High God, in the
words of our prayer, are called *to ventures of which we cannot see*
the ending, by paths as yet untrodden. That is just the way life is,

isn't it? This is true both in regard to locale as well as to life's circumstances. Several years ago Bishop Chilstrom said, "I have never been anywhere I expected to be." This has certainly been my experience, and I have a hunch you can relate to it as well, if not in locale, certainly in life's circumstances.

Fifty years ago this spring, as a personal example, I really wanted to attend St. Olaf College in Northfield, Minnesota. I applied but was turned down because of a post-war rush of their own ELC Norwegian veteran applicants of which I was not one. I, therefore, applied to and was accepted by my second choice, Wittenberg College in Springfield, Ohio. Far from being bitter about St. Olaf's rejection, I came to realize that this was the best thing that ever happened to me. You see, in God's providence a young pastor's daughter named Mary Fonda Setzer from Louisville, Kentucky, ended up with me on the same campus. Otherwise, we never would have met. I thank God that our lives thus intersected where I had never expected to be.

Then, when I was about to graduate from seminary, I did not give so much as a thought to returning to my own Illinois Synod of the then ULCA from which I had come. With a spirit of adventure coursing through me, I wanted to serve somewhere in new territory, but "out of the blue," Mary and I were called to begin our ministry here in Lena, a town of which I had never even heard. A few short years later I was pressured by the Synod President to preach a so-called "trial sermon" in Trinity Lutheran Church in Carthage, Illinois. Settled in and happy here in Lena, I spent the whole trip driving home from Carthage that day trying to figure out how to keep from going there. When after considerable anguish we did leave Lena, I was crying so hard as we drove out of town on Route 73 that I could scarcely keep the car on the road. Still, we followed the call of the Lord. Then after serving several good years in Carthage, I was invited to consider a church in suburban Philadelphia, a part of the country I had said in seminary that I would never go. I actually turned the congregation down, so reluctant was I to go there, but I was subsequently *forced* to reverse myself under *the onslaught of the Holy Spirit*. That is no exaggeration! After twenty years of service in that city neither my family nor I wanted to serve in the South, but over a period of months the call to Charlotte in North Carolina became ever more clear. When finally I was called to Robbinsdale in Minnesota, I was not a little unnerved knowing I would inherit some real problems in that church, that it could thus become a difficult and discouraging place to end my ministry, and that it presented an overwhelming responsibility perhaps beyond my strength and ability. Thus I had some second thoughts before finally accepting that call. *None* of these places were where we ever expected to be and *some* of these places were not even where we wanted to be but *all* of these places were where God called us to be. In the beginning of life I could not see where life would take me. Our opening prayer thus bespeaks profound truth when it states that as servants of the Lord God we are called *to ventures of which we cannot see the ending, by paths as yet untrodden.* We, therefore, certainly need the guidance of the Holy Spirit.

Then, along these *paths as yet untrodden*, as our prayer further states, we pass *through perils unknown.* Isn't that the truth? A few months ago I copied down a line from a television mini-series on the *Titanic.* It was spoken by a sailor to a surviving widow of that disaster as they stood by the rail of the *Carpathia*, the ship which rescued the survivors of the *Titanic.* He said to her, "It is good, ma'am, that we don't know how things are going to end in the beginning or we'd never make the journeys that we were meant to take in this life...." I don't want to press that statement too far, but the truth in it is worth considering.

Take marriage and the family. These parts of our lives can at times be unexpectedly difficult. Marriage starts out so beautifully in a lovely wedding ceremony, but the wedding service itself gives hints of what will inevitably follow. Many among us, for example, used the vow that included the words, "for better for worse, for richer for poorer, in sickness and in health." Though Mary and I have had a very good marriage and are still the best of friends loving each other more with every passing year, we have, nevertheless, had much of all of these things: better hours and worse hours, days of some prosperity and days when we could hardly make ends meet, times of ill health and times of robust health. Has not your experience been the same? Furthermore, in the *LBW* Order for Marriage, the pastor says, "Because of sin, our age-old rebellion, the gladness of marriage can be overcast...." Who here does not understand that? Moreover, though the birth of a child is an undisputed joy, the wedding service itself says, "the gift of the family can become a burden." And, people, we are never finished with parenting! As someone put it, "Parenthood is never over. You never get to do that touchdown dance in the end zone."

"The gladness of marriage can be overcast," so says the service, but sometimes *that* can be devastating. A beautiful 34-year-old Lutheran Sunday school teacher was crowned Mrs. Minnesota. As her stylist was brushing her lovely long blond hair the very day of the pageant, an unwelcome hunk of hair came out. The contestant remarked, "Well, that's a sign the chemo is working." Only the previous month, in her own words, her "life's path and dreams took a huge turn" as she was diagnosed with breast cancer. A mastectomy and chemotherapy followed. With her stage 3 cancer already in her lymph nodes, she herself said her chances were "real grim." (Sadly, Mary Kay Sanders died in February of 1998.) A dear 83-year-old widow, desperately missing her late beloved husband and terribly lonely, said recently, "I just don't have any happiness anymore. I wish God would come and take me." Perhaps most tragic of all, marriage can become loveless and sink like the *Titanic.* I will never forget a man poignantly saying in a church singles group, "I didn't get married to get divorced." We have all seen such things in the lives of those near and dear to us, and many now within the sound of my voice have personally experienced these things or something similar. Even the best of marriages are sometimes burdened by difficulties and heartache and tragedy. In marriage, as well as in all of life, no one can escape those inevitable *perils unknown.* We, therefore, certainly need to be buoyed up by the power of the Holy Spirit.

For all that, as I reflect back across my own 68 years, I would have to say that my life has been *beyond expectation* and certainly *beyond my deserving.* The joys and satisfactions I have known as a disciple of Jesus have far, far outweighed the trials and tribulations I have experienced as a human being. When I retired from the active ministry in 1993, I went out with a profound sense of gratitude to God Who has blessed my life and ministry. Moreover, even though there have been some tears along the way, I thank God for "the gladness of marriage" and "the gift of the family." I can therefore identify with something Cris Carter, the record-breaking wide receiver for the Minnesota Vikings, once said. This all-pro football player, who is also a Christian gentleman and an ordained minister, said this: "Sometimes I am in awe of what God has done with my life." My friends, there are challenging and exciting things out there on those *paths as yet untrodden* even though at times we must pass *through perils unknown.*

Still, when tough times come, and come they do, what do we *need* to make it through? What does it take in a congregation's life, in marriage and family life, and, yes, in our individual lives to cope with what may befall us? What we need, continuing in the words of our prayer, is the *faith to go out with good courage.* So confidently do we look up into the face of our Lord as we acknowledge to him, *your hand is leading us and your love supporting us.* Believe me, these two spiritual resources are enough to empower us to stand up to anything life can throw at us.

I

First, to quote our prayer again, **not knowing where we go, we can nevertheless go out with good courage because God's hand is leading us**. Remember, He can see farther and is fully able to lead us step by step as He walks with us on the journey of life. As 1939 was tumbling into 1940 and the lights were going out all over the world, King George VI of England stepped up to the BBC microphone and spoke these stirring words: "I said to the man who stood at the gate of the year, 'Give me a light, that I may tread safely into the unknown,' and he replied, 'Go out into the darkness and put your hand into the hand of God. That shall be to you better than light and safer than a known way.' " Some of us here are old enough to remember the horrors of World War II which followed. But now we know that God surely did lead the British Empire safely through.

Again and again in the Gospels, Jesus said to would-be disciples, "Follow me!" But he also promised on the Day of Ascension to walk right along with us, saying, *"I am with you always!"* (Matthew 28:20). Those apostles like Abraham before them "went out, not knowing whither [they] went," (Hebrews 11:8) but the Living Christ was always there to lead them. These witnesses of the resurrection had hardly a clue, as we have said, regarding either the *paths as yet untrodden* or the *perils unknown*. But later on, looking back on where they had been and the mine fields of life through which they had already walked, they understood what God had said to King David, "I have been *with you* wherever you went" — "... *with you* wherever you went!" Only the Holy Spirit can *enable us* to recognize that.

My friends, I call you to witness from my own life that I have often prayed for God's guidance, and though at times I have had to wait for the fullness of *His time* to hear a clear answer, it has, nevertheless, through the guidance of the Holy Spirit always come — *positively, definitely!* I'm not saying that the answer was written in the sky or that I heard a voice not audible to others, but I knew for sure when God had spoken. Now in my elder years with all my heart, I attest to the reality of Jesus' words, *"I am with you always!"* So I say to you this morning, put your hand into the hand of the Man from Galilee, and walk on with hope in your heart.

II

Second, **not knowing where we go**, in the words of our prayer again, we can nevertheless **go out with good courage** because **God's love is supporting us**. God's undiscourageable good will toward us supports us mightily as we pass through the maze of life. According to Scripture, though our "sins are like scarlet" because of God's love "they shall be as white as snow" (Isaiah 1:18 RSV). According to Scripture, though we may be tossed hither and yon by fierce winds and quaking earth, God's love gives us a footing upon which to stand so we can say with the Psalmist, "The Lord ... set my feet upon a rock, making my steps secure" (Psalm 40:2). According to Scripture, though we may die, God's love enables us to stare death in the face unflinchingly and say, "To live is Christ, and to die is gain" (Philippians 1:21 RSV). You see, God's love enables us to make it through anything and then at last brings us safely home.

God's love can take even *sin* and *adversity* and *death* and make music out of them. Do you know who wrote the hymn, "Amazing Grace"? It was John Newton, an immoral pagan who once left England to be free to sin more violently. Becoming then involved in the hideous slave trade, he was surprisingly and mercifully rescued by the Lord Jesus Christ. It was out of his own life's experience he wrote, *Amazing Grace, how sweet the sound, that saved a wretch like me!* Do you know who wrote the hymn "O Love that will not let me go"? It was George Matheson who as a young man lost his eyesight. To make matters worse, he was utterly crushed when his fiance then broke their engagement, but a loving Lord picked him up, dusted him off, and enabled him to keep on keeping on. Through his own tears, he wrote, *O Love that will not let me go, I rest my weary soul in thee!* Do you know who wrote the hymn, "Abide with me"? It was Henry Lyte, a robust man whose health nevertheless broke, causing years of suffering. Only days before he died of tuberculosis, he penned these immortal words out of his own suffering: *Abide with me, fast falls the even tide ... Swift to its close ebbs out life's little day.* Only the loving Spirit of Christ can *empower us* to come back at life with faith and courage like this.

Paul heard the Lord Jesus say to him, "My grace is sufficient for you" (2 Corinthians 12:9). In the New English Bible, however, the translation reads: "My grace is *all you need.*" Though Paul called himself the chief of sinners, he heard Jesus say, if you will, "My grace — my all-sufficient love — is *all you need.*" Though Paul faced many adversaries and much adversity in his ministry, he heard Jesus say, as it were, "My grace — my all-powerful love — is *all you need.*" Though Paul in the end had to wear the martyr's crown, he first heard Jesus repeatedly say in various ways, "My grace — my eternal love — is *all you need.*" *Sin, adversity,* and *death* — listen to the man roll back these age-old threats to humankind: To the Romans he wrote, "While we still were sinners Christ died for us" (5:8). Then to the Philippians he wrote, "I can do all things through [Christ] who strengthens me" (4:13). And to Timothy while at death's door he wrote triumphantly, "I have fought the good fight, I have finished the race, I have kept the faith" (2 Timothy 4:7). In summary, Paul wrote in Romans 8:39 that nothing "... in all creation, will be able to separate us from the love of God in Christ Jesus our Lord." Dear friends, such wondrous love is more than enough to see us safely through to life's end.

On a memorable flight from Philadelphia to St. Louis, though I never saw the pilot, I trusted him even though some rather unsettling things happened. First, while we sat in the plane waiting, the lights went out and the passengers had to sit there a long while in darkness. When the lights finally went back on, they went off once more. As I was wondering if something was dangerously wrong with the electrical system, the pilot's calm voice came over the speaker telling us they were having trouble with the external power system but that the plane itself was all right. Then a full half-hour after our scheduled departure, a fuel truck drove up under the wing and started fueling the plane. I wondered about that, for surely, I thought, they knew how much fuel it took to fly some eight hundred miles to St. Louis. I accepted the fact, however, that there must be some good reason why they had to add fuel. Once again, however, the pilot's reassuring voice came over the speaker system saying we would be leaving in a few minutes. Finally we took off a full hour late.

Ninety minutes later as we approached our destination, the calm voice of the pilot informed us that the St. Louis airport was fogged in though planes were still landing. The inference was that we would be the last plane in before they closed Lambert Field. I caught on, then, that the extra fuel was just in case we had to overfly St. Louis and land elsewhere. Even though I had never landed in dense fog before, the pilot was so calm and nonchalant that I reasoned he surely knew what he was doing. *So we began our descent.* After a while the wing flaps went down thus applying the aerial brakes. *Down and down we went!* Then the wheels were lowered and locked into place, slowing our speed even more. *Down and down we continued!* We were getting closer to the ground which I could not see through the thick blackness below. *Down and down we continued, going for a long while!* I knew by the length of the descent and the sound of the jet engines that we must be getting very close to the ground. *Down and down we went some more!* It occurred to me with some gratitude that there are no mountains in the St. Louis area. *Down and down we still kept going!* Then, all of a sudden, for one brief flickering moment, we could see headlights on the highway skirting the airport, and then in an instant the runway rose up to meet us with its welcoming lights and white strips. That pilot, assisted by radar and the tower, knew all along what he was doing. He had done it before. He could see what we could not see. He was experienced. So he brought us safely in.

Friend, God will likewise bring you safely in. Trust Him. My God, in whom I trust, has never let me down. From the vantage point of many years now, I have given you my witness this day that the good Lord has been with me both in good times and in tough times as long ago I gave my life to Jesus and have followed him ever since, so why should I not count on him *now* to bring me safely home? And to help you collectively as a congregation and individually as human beings, as it has helped me so much, I suggest you memorize this same prayer with which I begin my days. It is a prayer for all seasons, a prayer that covers all circumstances. Please turn with me to page 137 in the front of the *Lutheran Book of Worship*. At the bottom of page 137 there are three prayers. The one we have been talking about this morning is the one in the middle. Page 137. With deep meaning, let us pray this prayer of the day together.

> *Lord God, you have called your servants to ventures of which we cannot see the ending, by paths as yet untrodden, through perils unknown. Give us faith to go out with good courage, not knowing where we go, but only that your hand is leading us and your love supporting us; through Jesus Christ our Lord. Amen.*[1]

---

1. Prayer reprinted from *Lutheran Book of Worship*, copyright © 1978, by permission of Augsburg Fortress, p. 137.

Looking Back *Gratefully*
And Then Striding Onward *Faithfully*

An Address at a 125th Anniversary Banquet

Trinity Lutheran Church,
Carthage, Illinois
November 1, 1998

There is a Transfiguration hymn in the old *Common Service Book* which begins, "'Tis good, Lord, to be here!" That expresses how I feel today being with you on this special 125th anniversary Sunday. Moreover, I feel truly privileged and blessed to have once served this church as pastor. Now it is an honor to have been invited back for this occasion. Truly, my friends, "'Tis good to be here!"

When God called me to be Pastor of Trinity Lutheran Church over forty years ago, as some of you may well remember, not only was I still wet behind the ears, I was also scared to death of serving a college, town, and rural congregation like this. It was a scary challenge for a "kid pastor" who was still unsure of himself. For all that, you took me in, loved me, showed kindness to me, gave encouragement to me, prayed for me, had patience with me, and granted understanding to me. To this day, believe me, I am profoundly grateful. Furthermore, your examples of the Christian faith and life have been a consistent inspiration over the years. More than you can fully know, you helped me in my own spiritual journey and nourished me into a self-confidence I didn't come here with. All this helped prepare me for what was to come in my life as a Lutheran pastor. Over the years the difficulties of being a minister in times like these increased substantially, and the responsibilities I was called upon to bear grew considerably. Sometimes I was overwhelmed and even tempted to throw in the proverbial towel. At such times, I would remember that once there

61

was a church that believed in me even though I was young, inexperienced, and sometimes inept. I tell you this today, not as I ought, but as I am able and quoting the words of Paul to his favorite church at Philippi: "I thank my God every time I remember you." From the bottom of my heart, dear friends, I want to express to you my profound appreciation.

I also want to thank you for inviting my dear wife Mary to share with us on this auspicious occasion. At least three times, your chair went out of her way to make known that Mary was included in your gracious invitation. When I spoke in Trinity on the one hundredth anniversary in 1973, though you invited her, Mary was unable to make the trip from Philadelphia with me. All the more, therefore, do I appreciate having her by my side this day. She has been the love of my life now for nearly half a century. She has been my partner in marriage for nearly five decades. She has given me four wonderful children. She has made me better than I ever would have otherwise been. She has been my inspiration and my teacher. And in so many ways, she has brought beauty into my life. On the wall of my present study, there is a framed collage picturing the five churches we have served. Appropriately printed at the top in large letters are the words, "41 YEARS OF MINISTRY" with *both* of our names underneath. You see, we have been partners *also* in the calling of the Lord. We are and have been "One in the Spirit and One in the Lord!" In His loving providence, I am saying now as best I can, God gave me a far better wife than I ever deserved. Thank you Lord, and thank you, dear Mary!

As you know, we now live in a house we designed and built in southwestern Virginia in a town named Radford near one of our daughters and her family. Life has a strange way, doesn't it, in carrying us to places and into circumstances we never could have guessed at the beginning? Three years ago, I had never heard of a place called Radford, and I could not have located it on a map. Now we live there.

Reading again through your one hundredth anniversary booklet, I saw a picture which brought to mind a story of a small church out there in the nearby Blue Ridge Mountains of Virginia which, by the way, we can see from the windows of our house. They had a problem in that church. The problem was that the nave was poorly lighted: there were not enough windows to bring in outside light. On a rainy or cloudy day one could scarcely see to read the hymns. So they did what all good Lutheran churches do: they appointed a committee to look into the matter. The report came back in a timely manner suggesting a chandelier be hung in the nave similar to the two pictured here in Trinity's one hundredth anniversary booklet. Do you remember this picture? Trinity solved the lighting problem by hanging these chandeliers, you see, but this mountain church solidly voted the suggestion down. Three reasons were given in the congregational meeting where, of course, all the Lord's business is done. One reason was that nobody could spell the word. Another reason was that nobody knew what a chandelier is. And a third reason was, as one member put it, "What we really need here is *light!*"

Well, as this congregation has grown older and celebrated anniversaries, we ourselves have been accumulating birthdays. Though the outside of Trinity Church looks much the same as it always did, we humans tend to age and change in appearance. Perhaps I should have said that you all still look the same as you always did, but as you can see, I, at least, have grown older. When I served here I still had hair which was blond at that. Now I am grey-haired and pretty sparse on top. I also walk more slowly, get tired more quickly, and have been gobbled-up at times by quite a "forgettery."

I even occasionally get mixed up like five dear old ladies who were stopped by a State Police Officer. He had been sitting by the side of the highway with his radar gun waiting to catch speeding drivers when this car with the five ladies came puttering along at 22 miles an hour. Since the minimum speed on an interstate highway is 45, the officer turned on his lights and pulled the driver over. The ladies in the car were wide-eyed and white as ghosts. The driver, obviously confused, said to him, "Officer, I don't understand, I was doing exactly the speed limit. What seems to be the problem?" "Ma'am," the officer replied, "you weren't speeding, but you should know that driving slower than the speed limit can also be a danger to other drivers." "Slower than the speed limit? No, sir, I was doing the speed limit *exactly:* 22 miles per hour," the old woman said a bit proudly, pointing to a sign just ahead. The police officer, trying to contain a chuckle, explained to her that the "22" was the route number, not the speed limit. A bit embarrassed, the woman grinned and thanked the officer for pointing out her error. "But before I let you go, ma'am, I have to ask, is everyone in this car okay? These women seem awfully shaken up, and they haven't muttered a peep this whole time." "Oh, they'll be all right in a minute, officer. *We just got off Route 119.*"

I'm certainly glad to see many new members since my time as well as younger people here, but I want to share with you a birthday card my brother-in-law, Peter, sent me on my seventieth birthday. In the style of David Letterman, it lists the ten top hymns for people our age. They are as follows:

10. "It Is Well With My Soul" (but my back aches a lot)
 9. "Nobody Knows The Trouble I Have Seeing"
 8. "Amazing Grace" (considering my age)
 7. "Just A Slower Walk With Thee"
 6. "Count Your Many Birthdays, Name Them One By One"
 5. "Go Tell It On The Mountain" (and speak up!)
 4. "Give Me That Old Timer's Religion"
 3. "Blessed Insurance"
 2. *My own personal favorite:* "Guide Me, O Thou Great Jehovah" (I've forgotten where I parked)

And the number one hymn for people our age — seriously now — is ...

 1. "Nearer, My God, To Thee"

Today we are surrounded by a great cloud of witnesses who were and are near to the heart of God. They were sustained in this world and saved for the world to come as the Holy Spirit drew them *nearer to God* through the saving grace of Jesus Christ. "Under the shadow of [God's] throne, Your saints have dwelt secure." I do believe these dear departed loved ones and former Trinity members are looking in on us today and even enjoying the festivities. In the fullness of God's time, they have been called to that far, far better place reserved in Heaven for those who believe in Jesus Christ as Savior and Lord. In this world they were undergirded by God's presence, saved by the precious blood of Jesus Christ, and strengthened in the inner person by the Holy Spirit as, "They climbed the steep ascent of heav'n through peril, toil, and pain." At last they were carried to that heavenly place which Jesus has prepared for his faithful followers. I would love to mention names today, which come easily to mind, but I cannot for I am sure that I would inadvertently omit some appropriate names of "Old Trinity" saints who are still precious to those left behind. But you know and I know who these saints are. After these four decades I remember them well. I would like to pause right here, therefore, for a minute and lead you in the prayer for saints printed in the *Lutheran Book of Worship*. Please join me in prayer:

> *Lord God, you have surrounded us with so great a cloud of witnesses. Grant that we encouraged by the example of your servants whom we now silently name in our hearts* (pause) — *grant that we encouraged by their example may persevere in the course that is set before us, to be living signs of the Gospel and at last, with all the saints, to share in your eternal joy; through Jesus Christ our Lord. Amen.*[1]

Isn't that what churches are for? In the Church of Jesus Christ the Holy Spirit draws us ever *nearer to God* and gives us the blessed assurance of eternal life. Luther wrote in the *Small Catechism* that the Holy Spirit "calls, gathers, enlightens, and sanctifies the whole Christian Church on earth and keeps it united with Jesus Christ in the one true faith." In Trinity Church through all these *years* and in the "one holy catholic and apostolic Church" through all these *centuries*, the fellowship of believers has experienced the incomparable blessing of forgiveness, been given the strength to stand up and take it when at wits' end, and enabled at last to sing out with Simeon of old, "Lord, now lettest thou thy servant depart in peace" (KJV). This is what Trinity Church has been doing now for a century and a quarter.

Mark this: the Holy Spirit is the One Who draws us ever *nearer to God* through the Savior, Jesus Christ. As God's "only begotten Son" he says to us that which he has been saying to all people for nearly 2,000 years, "Come unto me!" he is saying to us now as long ago He said in the book of Revelation 3:20, "Behold, I stand at the door, and knock; if any man/any woman [will] hear my voice and open the door, I will come in ..." (KJV). And this same Jesus is reminding us all as he reminded the apostles on the Day of Ascension, "I am with you always." Hear that well: *I am with you! With you! With you!*

A few years ago I read the Bible through in the New English version. As I did, I underlined in red from start to finish the words, "I am with you." These four words and similar ones appear many, many times on the pages of Scripture. Check that out for yourself when you read the Bible. You see, we are not alone through the living of our years, my friends, for God is surely with us one by one as well as being right here in the midst of the fellowship of believers we know as the Christian Church. Especially He comes to us through the Word and Sacraments.

> *Nearer my God, to Thee!*
> *Nearer to Thee!*
> *Through Word and Sacrament*
> *Thou com'st to me.*

How true! It behooves us, therefore, continually to saturate ourselves in God's Word thereby making ourselves amenable to the Spirit of Christ. We need to read the Bible faithfully in our devotions. We need to listen to it regularly in church. We need to put special verses into our private memory box ready to be released in the hour of trial. We need to let the Word of God bring enlightenment and reinforcement to us in tough times. We need to let the Bible grow us in Christ and thus be brought ever *nearer to the Eternal God.* Many of us here have been thus receptive for decades.

Furthermore, we cannot live the Christian life without taking the Sacraments seriously. This is certainly true of the Sacrament of

Holy Baptism which is ever so much more than a one time ceremony. One of the prayers I keep in my Bible begins this way: "Lord God, when I get swallowed up in my own sin, doubting that anyone loves me, much less You, remind me to quote Luther: 'But I am baptized!' When it is necessary, Lord, when I am really discouraged with myself, and have no hope, remind me to say to myself again and again, like a litany: 'But I am baptized! But I am baptized!' In baptism, Lord God, I became your child, and now nothing can separate us from one another." Baptism brings us *nearer to the God you can count on.*

Holy Communion brings us *nearer to the God Who demonstrates a love that will not let us go.* At the foot of the Cross we hear Jesus say to us, "This is my Body, given for you. This is my Blood shed for you and for all people for the forgiveness of sin." Who among us confronted by such wondrous love does not thereby rise a better man, a better woman, a better child of God having been thus drawn *nearer to God.* I say, this is what "Old Trinity" has been about doing so splendidly all these years of her history. And this is what readies you and me for the Kingdom of Heaven to come.

Now we arrive at the conclusion which I offer today in three parts. The classic Lutheran sermon, as you know, has three points, but in a different twist today, I have a conclusion in three parts, each shorter than the one that precedes it.

First, I am pulling from my pocket a packet of 3 x 5 cards on which are typed verses of Scripture which, I believe, speak, a relevant word to us at such a time as this. When I finish reading these Bible verses, pausing now and then for meditation, I am going to just put the cards down here on the table. It may be some of you might want to pick one up and then perhaps the leftovers could be used as filler for the church bulletin or newsletter. But I am suggesting now that every one of these verses has something to say to us at this anniversary celebration.

> *The grass withers, the flower fades; but the Word of our God will stand forever.* (Isaiah 40:8)

Do this in remembrance of Me. (1 Corinthians 11:24)

If God be for us, who can be against us? (Romans 8:31 KJV)

I am the Lord ... I have taken you by the hand and kept you. (Isaiah 42:6)

When you pass through the waters, I will be with you; and through the rivers, they shall not overwhelm you; when you walk through fire you shall not be burned, and the flame shall not consume you. For I am the Lord your God. (Isaiah 43:2-3)

He gives power to the faint, and strengthens the powerless. (Isaiah 40:29)

The steadfast love of the Lord never ceases, his mercies never come to an end. (Lamentations 3:22)

The Lord is merciful and gracious, slow to anger and abounding in steadfast love ... [which] is from everlasting to everlasting. (Psalm 103:8, 17)

I, I am he who blots out your transgressions ... and I will not remember your sins. (Isaiah 43:25)

Far be it from me to glory except in the Cross of our Lord Jesus Christ. (Galatians 6:14 RSV)

One thing I do, forgetting what lies behind and straining forward to what lies ahead, I press on toward the goal for the prize of the upward call of God in Christ Jesus. (Philippians 4:13-14 RSV)

The one who endures to the end will be saved. (Matthew 24:13)

I am the resurrection and the life. Those who believe in me, even though they die, will live, and everyone who lives and believes in me will never die. (John 11:25-26)

I have fought the good fight, I have finished the race, I have kept the faith. (2 Timothy 4:7)

Be faithful unto death, and I will give you the crown of life. (Revelation 2:10)

The second conclusion is this: Pastor Robert Wandersee was one of the missionaries sponsored by our former congregation, Central Lutheran Church in Minneapolis. On August 7 of this year in Nigeria he was randomly attacked by robbers and shot and killed. The last word he whispered before he was shot, as reported by a survivor of the attack — the last word he uttered was "Jesus." One of our pastors at Central, where Pastor Wandersee was buried, knew him personally. He wrote in the church newsletter, "Bob knew he had to deny himself many comforts when he took up the cross to follow Jesus as a missionary. He was aware that 'those who save their life will lose it and those who lose their life for Jesus' sake will find it.' The robbers asked Bob what he was hiding when he was pressing the bullet wounds on his shoulder with his bloodied hands. He opened his hand to show he was hiding nothing, but giving [his] all, even his life."

Doesn't that remind you somewhat of the first pastor of this church, Dr. David Tressler, who simultaneously served as President of Carthage College? There was that February afternoon and night in 1880 when, after preaching in "Old Trinity" in the morning, Dr. Tressler insisted on going the twelve miles to West Point to preach in the evening. Since the roads were too bad to go by horse and buggy, Dr. Tressler travelled the distance by horseback even though it was quite cold and damp. He returned late that evening very fatigued and chilled to the bone. Subsequently he developed a severe cold that soon turned into pneumonia. He died less than three weeks later at the age of 41.

Thus Robert Wandersee and David Tressler gave their all to Jesus Christ, the King of kings and Lord of lords. *But what a morning followed their untimely deaths!* They entered into the Kingdom of Heaven and saw their Lord and Savior, Jesus Christ, face to face.

Take they then our life,
Goods, fame, child, and wife,
When their worst is done,
They yet have nothing won:
The Kingdom ours remaineth.

And now, this final conclusion: If I don't see you again in this world, I'll see you in Heaven. God bless you one and all.

---

1. Prayer reprinted from *Lutheran Book Of Worship*, copyright © 1978, by permission of Augsburg Fortress, p. 36.

What Gives Commitment Staying Power

A Sermon at the First Churchwide Assembly of the ELCA

Chicago, Illinois
August 24, 1989

We will not agree on everything at this assembly but one thing
I think we might agree on is that church work is hard — usually
satisfying, often joyful, but *hard*! So what else is new? Not for nothing did Paul write to young Timothy, "Endure hardness, as a good
soldier of Jesus Christ" (KJV). When we grow "weary in well-doing," when stress does its best to burn us out, when our sinful nature
betrays us, when budget pressures sap our energy, when difficulties
mount, when enthusiasm wanes — what then? When a synodical
official said, ineloquently, "Church work ain't easy!" he was not
even saying the half of it. Whatever else it takes to survive in the
service of the Lord, therefore, it takes commitment.

How refreshing it is when our Bishop boldly and unapologetically uses this significant word in his vision for our Church
called *Mission90*. He confronts us with the simple yet profound
question, "What does it mean to be a Christian?" He challenges us
as individuals, as congregations, and as a Church to be committed
to *see*, to *grow*, and to *serve*. Consequently, the Church Council is
calling upon this assembly to endorse a statement of commitment
and upon the ELCA to carry it through.

In so doing, it seems to me we are rescuing the word "commitment" from the semantic doghouse. We Lutherans have shied away
from that word, haven't we, and with some justification. Many
Christians have tended to make commitment a human-centered
concept, as though it were only something *we* did. Granted, sometimes we can just say, "No!" and thereby avoid doing wrong. Occasionally, we can even say "Yes!" and do some things right — for
a while. But what is it that enabled Paul, with all his trials, nevertheless to carry through to a strong finish where he could exclaim

71

triumphantly, "I have fought the good fight, I have finished the race, I have kept the faith!" (2 Timothy 4:7)? There is much more to commitment, you see, than *won't-power* and *will-power.* But what?

The clue is in the concluding words of today's text from Isaiah 58: "Then you shall call, and the Lord will answer; you shall cry for help, and He will say, *'Here I am!'* " That's it! This Old Testament pericope rises in a crescendo which concludes with God speaking three powerfully encouraging words: "Here I am!" *My friends, what gives our commitment staying power is the abiding presence of God!* I suspect someone here needs to hear that said.

When the London Missionary Society asked David Livingstone where he would like to go, he responded, "Anywhere!" Listen to this prayer recorded in his diary: "Lord, send me anywhere, *only go with me.* Lay any burden on me, *only sustain me.*" So they sent him to Africa. There he was severely tested. He was frequently separated from his family and ultimately buried his wife in the midst of that continent. He suffered bouts with tropical diseases. He faced the spears of hostile tribesmen and the roaring of wild beasts. He was half-chewed up by a lion that all but ripped his left arm from his body. So what kept him going? What was the secret of his commitment? The answer is in something he said to the students at the University of Glasgow: "Shall I tell you what sustained me," he asked rhetorically in this address. "Shall I tell you what sustained me in the midst of all these toils and hardships and incredible loneliness? It was the promise of a gentleman of the most sacred honor; it was this promise, 'Lo, I am with you alway, even unto the end of the world' " (Matthew 28:20 KJV). David Livingstone remained faithful to the finish, being buried at last with honor in Westminster Abbey. God in Christ *powerfully* underlines and accentuates our text from Isaiah wherein we hear God saying simply, "Here I am!" There is enough potency in these three little words to rally our Church and to enable us to "go from strength to strength."

In Psalm 59:10 in the King James Version, there is an intriguing verse that initially seems quite irrelevant and even boring. It reads, "The God of my mercy shall prevent me." What in the world does that mean? We come closer to the meaning when we remember the word "prevent" actually means "go before," so that a better and quite accurate translation of the verse is this: "My God in His lovingkindness shall meet me at every corner." I like that: "My God in His lovingkindness shall meet me at every corner." He is there at the "corners" of life to meet us, and this is what He says: "Here I am!"

We come to many "corners" in our church work, don't we, where it helps to know that God is there, in His lovingkindness, saying for our encouragement, "Here I am!" There is that "corner" "of incredible adjustment" where, in a merger of three church bodies into the ELCA, there has been a galaxy of transitional and financial problems. My sisters and brothers in general church work, give an ear and hear the bracing words of God Himself saying, *Here I am willing to walk you through this one!* There is that "corner" at which sooner or later every conscientious clergyperson and church worker arrives, the corner of burnout that tends so to wear down and wear out a commitment. Have you never wondered how long you can stand the strain? Has it never seemed that all your efforts were being wasted and leading nowhere? Take heart, my friend. God is marching on, and He is saying this: *Here I am anxious to breathe new life into you!* There is the "corner" of local congregational problems, like a building program sometimes, where harebrained opinions come out of the woodwork, where intransigent church members get their backs up, where good people become like loose canons, and where a fund-raising drive gets so close to the pocketbook nerve that some folks panic. Have any of you ever been there? Well, "When these things begin to take place, stand up and raise your heads" — for Heaven is bending low and the Eternal God is speaking a relevant word to hearten us, saying, *Here I am ready to build a bridge into the future!*

At just such a trying time, though of far greater consequence, God broke into the world afresh at Bethlehem. If and when our commitment to Jesus Christ and his Church gets a bit wobbly and worn down, if our service in the King's Business starts to look bleak and hopeless, it is well to remember the despair at the time of Christ's birth. Over 35 years ago I took a course under Paul Tillich in Existential Philosophy. One lecture stands out vividly. It was a lecture on the mood of Greek philosophy which, he said, spilled down into the time when Christ was born. Dr. Tillich paralleled this mood to the wrath of God as expressed in Psalm 90 and the vanity of life of which we read in Ecclesiastes. He stated that the pre-Christian period was one of profound pessimism, quoting one of the ancients as saying, "No mortal man is happy and all whom the sun looks down on are miserable." He said the era was characterized by a universal feeling of emptiness. He reminded us that tumbling into the thinking of the day from the great Greek tragedies was the burden of inescapable guilt. At the end of this depressing lecture, the student next to me almost gasped — I shall never forget it! — he almost gasped, "You can really see what Christianity was up against!" At precisely such a time, however, God said in a unique and profound way, "Here I am!" and Christ was born. "When the fullness of time had come, God sent His Son, born of a woman ..." (Galatians 4:4). And, "The Word became flesh and dwelt among us ..." (John 1:14 RSV) bringing hope, fulfillment, and redemption as God profoundly said to that despairing generation as He is saying now to ours: "Here I am!"

And how did this happen? God came to a consecrated village girl, an ordinary person like us, a maiden who was willing to put herself into God's hands and stay with it. When called upon to be used by God, Mary humbly responded, "Behold, I am the handmaid of the Lord; let it be to me according to your word" (Matthew 1:38). That is the beautiful equivalent of "Thy will be done." So "Jesus Christ ... was conceived by the power of the Holy Spirit." When Joseph became concerned about Mary's pregnancy, an angel told him that Mary's child would be called "Emmanuel" (which means, God with us) which is saying the same thing our text is saying today: "Here I am!" It is worth noting, too, despite some questions along the way, that Mary the Mother of our Lord was still there at the *end* — at Calvary; and she was there, too, at the *beginning* — at Easter and at Pentecost. God was with Mary as He is with us now, sustaining our commitment to Jesus Christ and his Church.

My friends, God in His lovingkindness, meets us at every "corner" of life to say, "Here I am!" thus giving our commitment *staying power.* What a God — ours! Listen! He is "able to keep (us) from falling" (Isaiah 40:31). He bears "(us) on eagles' wings" (Jude 1:24 RSV). He says, "Stand up on your feet, and I will speak with you" (Ezekiel 2:1 RSV). And if we be like those dry bones, "He will put breath into (us), and (we) shall live; and (we) shall know that (He) is the Lord" (Ezekiel 37:6). He enters into our lives to "strengthen (us) with might through His Spirit in the inner man, the inner woman" (Ephesians 3:16). And through His only Son, He is saying still, "Lo, I am with you always...." God reinforces us, helps us, sustains us — drawing near at precisely those "corners" of life when we need the most to hear Him say, "Here I am!"

One of the most poignant scenes in motion pictures occurs near the end of the classic film of Tolstoy's *War and Peace.* Standing in what was left of the family's fire-mutilated Moscow mansion, Natasha says to the hard-hit and wounded Pierre, "You are like this house. You suffer. You show your wounds. But you stand!" *"But you stand!"* Likewise God keeps us standing by His abiding presence enabling us to make it through to the finish!

75

Reflections After Forty Years As A Lutheran Pastor

A Sermon Preached on the Fortieth Anniversary of Ordination

Elim Lutheran Church
Robbinsdale, Minnesota
May 31, 1992

Forty years ago this month I was ordained a pastor in the Lutheran Church. Along with twelve other candidates I was ordained on the night of May 14, 1952, in St. John's Lutheran Church in Joliet, Illinois. Through these years, I have been privileged to serve in five great congregations including Elim Lutheran Church here in Robbinsdale, Minnesota. As the Holy Spirit has guided me, I have not served anywhere I ever expected to be.

Before the ordination service the then President of the Illinois Synod, Dr. Harmon J. McGuire, suggested that each year on the anniversary of our ordination we should quietly withdraw somewhere, re-read the ordination service, and ponder anew the meaning of ministry. I have faithfully done this, and this anniversary is no exception. This year I re-read the ordination service out of the old *Common Service Book* four times, one for each decade. We were in Florida on vacation on May 14, and I read that service at dawn, at sunset, in the morning on the beach, and in the evening on a sailing vessel. Each time I thought and prayed my way through the service itself and all it meant when that night years ago I was publicly asked if I were willing to take upon myself the Holy Ministry with all it entailed. I answered individually as did each of the ordinands in turn, "Yes, with my whole heart, the Lord helping me through the power and grace of His Holy Spirit!"

Following through on the Lord's call to be a pastor and the Lord's commission to go and make disciples, I have baptized over one thousand babies and confirmed nearly 2,000 young people. As a matter of fact, for years back in Pennsylvania we had to have two

77

confirmation services a year because of such large classes. For quite a few of those years on a Wednesday I taught confirmation five times. I have preached the saving gospel of our Lord Jesus Christ on at least 2,000 occasions. Furthermore, more than half of my ministry, about 22 years, I have preached three times a Sunday. I have stood before the altar of God and received into the membership of the five churches I have served literally thousands of new members. I have administered the Holy Communion to a countless number of humble souls who have knelt to receive the Body and Blood of our Lord given and shed for the forgiveness of sins. I have also officiated at hundreds of weddings and stood by hundreds of open graves. In short, there has been considerable pastoral and prophetic ministry during these forty years as a Lutheran pastor.

In remembrance of all these things and thinking my way back through these forty years as well as ahead into the future, I trust this morning you will allow me to reminisce and reflect a bit. It may well be through the preaching of this sermon we here in Elim Church may be able to view afresh the precious gospel ministry in which we are partners in the Church of Jesus Christ and servants together of the Most High God.

First, when we pause to ponder it, the changes that have taken place during these past forty years have been nothing less than astounding.

Friends, it is a far different world now than it was then. When I was ordained in 1952, Harry Truman was still President. Since that time our country has seen eight presidents. In 1952 the four-minute mile had not yet been run, Mount Everest had not yet been climbed, Sputnik had not yet been launched, and polio had not yet been conquered. Moreover, many things which are now common-place were then either non-existent or so rare we hardly knew them such as color television, air conditioned cars, direct long-distance dialing, and jet passenger planes.

More particularly, many things have changed in the Church. Never expecting to have a salary as large as $10,000 a year and wondering if anybody could even be a Christian and make that kind of money, I was called to my first church at a salary of $3,000.

I also received a $420 auto allowance and a $300 utility allowance for our large 1872 vintage parsonage. I was ordained into the United Lutheran Church in America, the ULCA. Subsequently, because of church mergers, I have served in the Lutheran Church in America, the LCA, and now I serve in the Evangelical Lutheran Church in America, the ELCA. Over these four decades I have led worship out of three hymnals: the black *Common Service Book*, the red *Service Book and Hymnal*, and now the green *Lutheran Book of Worship*. When I entered the ministry, we used the King James Version of the Bible for readings in church. Shortly thereafter the Revised Standard Version was instituted and used for many years. Now we read the Scripture from the New Revised Standard Version. The first years in the ministry I wore a black robe to officiate at worship, then a black cassock with a white surplice over it, and now a white alb. Then the members of the congregation cooled themselves with fans supplied by the local funeral director; now most churches are air conditioned. Then we just talked as loudly as necessary to be heard; now even smaller churches have an audio system to boost the preacher's voice. Then we had Synod Presidents; now we have Bishops. And these are just a few of the many changes I have seen in our Lutheran Church during these years.

This leads to a further observation — namely, it is harder to be a pastor in 1992 than it was in 1952. To put it positively, which is my inclination, it is even more challenging to be a Christian lay person or a Christian clergy person now than it was then which means that, more than ever, you and I need to depend on Almighty God.

Many of you could identity with this in your own personal lives and occupations. In general, life is more complicated and stressful nowadays; there are more external pressures impacting upon our lives than in bygone years. It also seems that in life there are more innocent people being wounded and scapegoated and caused to suffer than years ago. Some of you have read Scott Peck's best-selling book, *The Road Less Travelled*. Do you remember the first sentence? It is this: "Life is difficult." Who among us would dispute that?

What I want to underscore here, however, is that it is harder, much harder to be a pastor in the '90s than it was in the '50s. No less than Lyle Schaller, the number one church consultant in the nation, has said the same. In the introduction to a recent book, he states the premise of the entire book in these words: "It is a different world today, and it is far more difficult to be a pastor in today's world than it was as recently as the 1950s." The title of the first chapter is, "It's Harder Today!" He then proceeds to list and explain sixteen reasons why it is harder to be a pastor in such a generation as ours. It seems to me in these times we clergy are right back where Saint Paul was when he wrote to the Corinthians about being "afflicted in every way ... perplexed ... persecuted ... struck down ..." (2 Corinthians 4:8-9). I understand that. I also understand where Paul was coming from when he wrote elsewhere of being "under daily pressure because of [his] anxiety for all the churches" (2 Corinthians 11:28). As one pastor put it after twenty years in one congregation, "I often wonder how I got through them. Whether my nerves would much longer stand the strain seemed at times questionable." My brothers and sisters in the clergy would agree that such feelings are more prevalent these days than several decades ago.

Thinking back across these challenging years, I thank God for those faithful lay persons who stood beside me, who were supportive of me, and who included me in their prayers. By God's grace, I have survived much stress and strain in the ministry and the weightiness of being a senior pastor since 1965. Honesty compels me to give God all the credit for this. Friends, ours is a very great God who can be trusted, who can be depended upon, and who will never let us down.

We'll pursue this thought shortly, but first another reflection. It is appropriate right here in the middle of this sermon to tell you how many wonderful laughs we have enjoyed along the way. Humor often relieves the stress and helps keep perspective. I thank God for this gift. It is one of God's graces.

Some years ago I returned to visit my first parish, and with the blessing of the current pastor I did a bit of visiting around. I recall in particular visiting a farm family and sitting on their back porch talking and reminiscing about our years together in that church. Among other things, we spoke of some fun times and practical jokes. As we talked the farmer's wife said to me, "I'd forgotten how many laughs we had when you were here as our pastor." I liked that! I suppose at times I have been too serious, but I have certainly enjoyed much laughter through these years.

For example, in the mid-'60s a parishioner actually told me he was embarrassed to belong to a church where the senior pastor drove such a dilapidated old car. Finally when that car gave up the ghost and literally had to be hauled off to the junk yard, we purchased a previously-used Chevrolet that looked like new. Mary and I decided to have some fun with this. Along with the car we received the original window price sticker. Knowing that the congregation would be curious to know just how much their preacher had squandered on such a car, we took great delight in imaginatively doctoring up that sticker. If I do say so myself, we did quite a good job, and it looked real. I taped this price sticker inside the rear window and parked the car in my reserved spot by the church the next Sunday morning. I knew most people, like me, would be curious to see how much the car cost. We typed a total price on the bottom of that piece of paper that was high enough to catch their instant attention. Sure enough, as we looked out through the church window between services, people would casually check the total price and then, being astounded by how much they thought their preacher had paid for this car with their dollars, they would inevitably check out what that price included. The first few items we listed with the costs were quite legitimate, but then we typed in such outrageous equipment as, a quick-starting 500 horsepower supercharged motor, a back seat television which they actually looked in the rear window to see, and retractable dual machine guns mounted in the front fenders. Some people even walked up to the front of the car to see that! Of course, the people caught on that it was a joke, but that gave us all many good laughs together, and the congregation never did know how much we paid for the car.

Seriously, someday I hope to write a book on the funny things that have happened, or we have "created," during our service in the church. I plan to tell in detail stories like this one about the car, another story about the mouse that came to church one rainy Sunday and casually walked down the center aisle causing pandemonium, another story to explain why one Sunday when people knelt to take communion they actually began one by one to laugh, another story about some committee minutes I had a good time writing as secretary and which even provided Synod officials with some hearty laughs, as well as many other stories. The truth is I don't think I could have made it through these stress-filled years without God's good gift of laughter.

More seriously now, amid the many formidable challenges and overwhelming responsibilities, and also amid personal and congregational trials which sometimes have swirled around me, any of which might well have torpedoed my faith, I want to say this loudly and clearly: my God in whom I trust has steadfastly sustained and upheld me. With the Psalmist I can say with all my heart, "I had fainted, unless I had believed" (Psalm 27:13 KJV).

This is my testimony: I want everyone to know that more than ever I am still confident in Christ. I celebrate with you today the practical resources of the Christian Faith. The Eternal God is not dead; He is alive and well. Even as long ago He sent His Son into the world to rescue us from sin and fling wide the gates of Heaven, just so, now together with His Son He sends the Holy Spirit to strengthen us in our inner being, to make us victors over life instead of life's victims, and to give us staying power. None of us can generate power enough to stand up to life. None of us can create power enough to see life through to a triumphant finish. No! We can only *receive* power. So vital faith in God is like a deep well that never runs dry. I tell you good people, God is right beside us to help us whatever our need may be. This is my testimony. I am still confident in Christ. Herbert Hoover, who was knocked around a good deal by people and life circumstances, was able to say, "My faith has helped me all through life." With all my heart I bear witness to the same.

Next this further reflection on these forty years of service as a Lutheran pastor: I am simply overwhelmed with gratitude to Almighty God.

82

I am awed and humbled and grateful that the Eternal God Who, though "... from everlasting to everlasting" (Psalm 103:17), has chosen to call me to be His servant in the Church. Though I am certain of His call I have often, nevertheless, asked, "Lord, why me?" I can identify with the hesitation and surprise of Moses, Isaiah, Jeremiah, Peter, and Paul. Particularly in the beginning I was quick to use some of their same excuses. It was during my freshman year in college when I finally stopped running away and surrendered to God's call. I have often compared my struggle with this call to trying to get away from God who all the while was holding on to the back on my suspenders to keep me from getting away. I'm glad He won, and now, despite many a trial along with much heartfelt joy in His service, I can join with another Lutheran pastor in exclaiming, "If I had a hundred lives to live, I'd be a minister one hundred times!"

I am also thankful to God for the churches I have been privileged to serve — all five of them. I have been very fortunate in the congregations to which I have been called to serve. Were time of no concern this morning, I could talk quite a long while about the things I appreciate in each of these five congregations. Here I would just like to say that, with the help of Almighty God, I have tried my best to be faithful.

I am also thankful to have served in ministry with some tremendous colleagues, both clergy and lay. Numerically speaking there have been many more lay members in these five congregations who have joined with me to advance the cause of Jesus Christ. Paul expressed it for me, too, when he wrote to the people of the church at Philippi, "I thank my God every time I remember you ... because of your sharing of the gospel ..." (Philippians 1:3, 5). These men and women through these years have worked with me, prayed with me, encouraged me, supported me, and, yes, criticized me. My critics, you see, have sometimes been my teachers. Years ago I read a novel on this subject by Lloyd C. Douglas titled, *Disputed Passage*. On one of the front pages, he quoted these words of Walt Whitman: "Have you learned lessons only of those who admired you, and were tender with you, and stood aside for you? Have you not learned great lessons from those who braced themselves against you and disputed the passage with you?" But thank God, these critics were always more than balanced by those dear friends and supporters who stood alongside of me in difficult times and joined with me as partners in the gospel.

And now quickly two end thoughts:

Before I finish, I want to remind you of the constancy of the gospel. We recognize this in our biblical theme for this year's seventieth anniversary of Elim Church: "Jesus Christ is the same yesterday and today and forever" (Hebrews 13:8). That is a tremendous thought! I read recently of a boy going to a teacher to take a music lesson. Upon arriving, he asked in a light-hearted way, "What is the good news today?" Without so much as saying a word, that teacher walked over to a tuning fork suspended from the ceiling and plucked it. "That, my son," he said "is the note 'A.' In this changing world, that is one thing that will not change. The sound you just heard has always been the note 'A,' and it always will be. You can count on it. And that is today's good news." So it is with the Good News of the gospel. The saving gospel of Jesus Christ is "the same yesterday and today and forever." Christ is where the gospel begins and where it ends. The whole thing is about him. He walks across the pages of Holy Scripture and out into our lives to save us from our sins, to deliver us from evil, and to open the gateway to the Kingdom of Heaven. Maybe you will recall that in my second sermon here as your senior pastor I preached on this text: "For I decided to know nothing among you except Jesus Christ, and him crucified" (1 Corinthians 2:2). That is what I have been called to proclaim through these four decades, and I have done my best to do just that.

Also before I finish, I want to express publicly my profound gratitude to my dear wife, Mary. She has been my constant companion, my helper, and my soulmate on this journey through both days of tears and days of joy. When life wasn't funny, she comforted me. When I was tempted to think of myself more highly than I ought to have thought, she punctured my balloon. When I would become discouraged and frustrated, she quoted to me what Bambi's father said to the young buck when danger threatened, "Get up, Bambi!" When it was time to rejoice, she was right there with me. It is hard for me to imagine what being a pastor these forty years would have been like without her. She has been my "Anselmo," a character in a poignant story by A. J. Cronin which someday I may try to read to you if I can get through it without tears. For all this and much more I would be remiss were I not to tell her personally and to tell you publicly how thankful I am for her love and friendship and her partnership with me in the gospel. Today after church we are going away to one of those romantic Minnesota inns as a gift from our children where tomorrow in our quiet way we will celebrate together and alone our fortieth wedding anniversary. Through all these years I thank God for her blessed companionship.

For these reasons and many more which there is no time left to state, I conclude with the uplifting words of the Psalmist, "O give thanks unto the Lord; for He is good!" (Psalm 118:1 KJV). Amen!

The Deadly Sin Of Sabotage

A Lenten Sermon Written but Never Preached

*One thing I do know, that though I was blind, now I
see. (John 9:25)*

Though they are nowhere specifically mentioned together in
the Bible, traditional theology has long maintained that there are
seven deadly sins. Just to refresh your memory, these seven sins
are pride, covetousness, lust, anger, gluttony, envy, and sloth. Sabotage is not one of these seven sins, and, in fact, the word "sabotage" does not even occur in the Bible.

I maintain, however, that sabotage is deadly to the souls of the
perpetrators as well as to the victims. Gamaliel said to his colleagues in Acts, "... you may even be found *fighting against God*!"
You can't do that and win! Sabotage can also be destructive, even
devastating, to victims, which includes worthy causes. Such can
cause good people to wobble in their trust in God and sometimes
even fall into disbelief. Not a few of us have sometimes been guilty
of committing this deadly sin, and not a few of us have also been
victimized by it. Thereby our spiritual well-being has been cast
into jeopardy. If we, therefore, can honestly face these hard facts,
perhaps we can find some remedies for this sin. Without apology,
therefore, I title this sermon, appropriately, "The Deadly Sin Of
Sabotage."

Understand at the outset that I am *not* referring here to war-
time sabotage. That is an altogether different subject. I'm referring
rather to the kind of everyday sabotage which is pervasive in society and even invades the Church which is the subject of the sermon
that follows. Many of us have had to face this "deadly sin," sometimes with agony of heart.

Webster's third definition of sabotage — not the first — is as
follows: "the deliberate obstruction of or damage to any cause, movement, activity, [or] effort...." Broadly speaking, again according to

Webster, sabotage is "any act or process tending to hamper or hurt." It is, as other students of the word's meaning have suggested, the undermining of a cause or person, the underhanded interference in a process, the attempt to damage something or somebody from inside the organization, the effort to cripple a worthwhile cause or to do a person in, the disruption of something that can well be good. This is serious stuff which we dare not brush aside. The weapons of the saboteur are such things as *deliberate deceit, smiling and being pleasant while figuratively stabbing someone in the back, letting the ego's desire run rampant to the detriment of others, ruthlessly trying to get the upper hand at all costs, undermining someone or something in every way possible, talking out of both sides of one's mouth and/or lying through one's teeth.* Never mind that sabotage is sometimes done unconsciously. It still hurts! It is still damaging! And it can still be as deadly as a serpent's tooth! I almost dread to make this meaning of sabotage as clear to you as it is to some of us who have been wounded by it personally and who have seen the things to which we have given our lives severely damaged by such underhandedness.

When some years ago I first discussed the possibility of a sermon on sabotage, my dear wife said to me in essence, "But, husband, dear, there is nothing in the Bible about sabotage." With all due respect to my beloved wife, it is just not so. The more I have read the Bible the more examples I have found of precisely what we are thinking about here. In fact, biblical instances of sabotage are legion.

In the Old Testament, for example, there is the sad story of David the King and his son Absalom, who, envisioning himself in his father's place, devised plans to usurp his father's throne. *Succumbing to insatiable ambition: that is frequently a component of sabotage!* A handsome young man without blemish from "the sole of his foot to the crown of his head," Absalom went out of his way to steal the hearts and loyalties of the people of Israel. Rising early in the morning, he would stand at the gates of Jerusalem charming the people, giving them what they wanted and telling them what they wanted to hear, while at the same time, he was plotting against his own father. His underhanded sabotage resulted eventually in outright civil war with his father the king in which Absalom himself was killed. That, the ultimate price, was what he paid for this deadly sin. But do hear also the deep agony of soul in King David as he wept bitter tears upon losing his son even as he thought about what might have been. In one of the most poignant outcries in the entire Bible, David cried out from the depths of his innocent suffering, "O my son Absalom, my son, my son, Absalom! Would that I had died instead of you, O Absalom, my son, my son!" You see, both David *and* Absalom suffered much because of this deadly sin.

Again from Scripture, there is neither space nor time here to tell the full story of the sabotage of the great prophet, Jeremiah, whom God Himself had sent to rescue the Children of Israel from their waywardness. Note the sabotage as his adversaries began to resent the truth the prophet was called upon by God Himself to proclaim. Consequently, his enemies were out to get him. Listen to the prophet as he begins to see what was going on, "I was like a gentle lamb led to the slaughter, and I did not know it was against me that they devised schemes ..." (19). That from the eleventh chapter of the book that bear's the prophet's name, this now from the eighteenth chapter: Then they [his enemies] said, "Come, let us make plots against Jeremiah" (18). *Conceiving of a plot: this is often a component of sabotage!* And this was done to one whose mouth had been touched by God and to whom God had said, "Now I have put my words in your mouth" (Jeremiah 1:9).

Still again from the Old Testament, there is the story of Nehemiah who set himself to a most worthy task, that is, rebuilding the walls of Jerusalem a century and a half after they had been destroyed by the Babylonians. Nehemiah's problem was that he was succeeding at this noble task, something that almost always generates enemies, for there were those who did not want the walls rebuilt. Those who wanted to keep the city in disgraceful ruins watched intently for any chance to thwart his efforts. They "mocked and ridiculed" his efforts. In fact, so it stands written in the book of Nehemiah, "They were very angry, and all plotted together to come and fight ... and to cause confusion" (4:8). *Engendering confusion: that is not at all an unusual component of sabotage!* They threatened him and tried to trick him so they could kill him, but Nehemiah boldly answered, "Should a man like me run away?" (Nehemiah 6:11). Then they sent letters deliberately crafted to intimidate him. In every way they knew how, they tried to sabotage Nehemiah's efforts, but nevertheless, the job was done in the amazingly short time of 52 days, and the walls were properly dedicated.

Crossing over into the New Testament, we find many more biblical examples of sabotage. The most important examples, of course, are found in the passion story which led to the crucifixion of Christ. We will return to this pivotal thought before we are finished with this lengthy sermon. *Executing a plan to do someone in: that can be a primary component of sabotage!* But New Testament sabotage by no means stops with this.

Stephen, for instance, who was to become the first martyr of the Church, was "full of [so much] grace and power," so we are told, that "they could not withstand the wisdom and the Spirit with which he spoke" (Acts 6:10). That was a formula for opposition and trouble. So what did his enemies do? They sabotaged him, that's what! "They stirred up the people" and when they brought him before the council, "They set up false witnesses." *Getting people steamed up about the wrong things: that is a common component of sabotage!* In the end they did him into death, but what they did against this good man from start to finish was an act of sabotage. Let us frankly call it what it is. Moreover, except for the notable example of Saul of Tarsus, there may well have been others there that day casting the stones who simultaneously cast their souls into hell.

Furthermore, the Apostle Paul was sabotaged in many ways by many people. Paul, as you will remember, began his first missionary journey by preaching and witnessing to the people in Galatia. He was then followed around that province by the so-called Judiazers, those Jewish Christians who so wanted to preserve Jewish customs that they did their level best to undercut the truth which Paul had proclaimed so compellingly about the gospel of Jesus Christ and Christian freedom. *Subverting the truth: that is a paramount component of sabotage!* Those Judiazers bent their whole-hearted efforts to sabotage the good work the apostle had done. Listen, therefore, to the response of Paul writing to the Galatians in blistering sentences: "I am astonished that you are so quickly deserting the one who called you in the grace of Christ and are turning to a different gospel — not that there is another gospel, but" — I'm still quoting the Bible here — "there are some who are confusing you and want to pervert the gospel of Christ. But even if we or an angel from heaven should proclaim to you a gospel contrary to what we proclaimed to you, let that one be accursed!" (Galatians 1:6-8). Hard words, these, written in white heat by Paul who, for Christ's sake, had felt the bitter sting of sabotage. And through it all the very salvation of human beings was at stake!

Before we go on to consider the devastating effect of sabotage in the modern Church, which is where this sermon is heading, let us consider two examples as to how this deadly sin works its way out in everyday life.

Sabotage surely shows its ugly head in the world of business and commerce. A friend of mine, let's call him Jeremy though that is not his name, built up a very successful commercial office supply business. Because he had business acumen and worked exceedingly hard, he was making significant money as the business grew and prospered. Jeremy then hired two men to work for him who came to the business with appropriate backgrounds and skills. He paid them both good money and added to that exceedingly generous benefits. They even received a Christmas bonus *and also* a profit sharing check in the spring. So to speak, Jeremy was the goose that laid the golden egg as the business continued to prosper. Business was, in fact, unbelievable! So what? So these two salesmen, for their own gain, began to sabotage him, that's what! *Putting selfish gain front and center: that is a fundamental component of sabotage!*

As owner and benefactor of these employees, Jeremy started to hear from his loyal customers that he should watch the business ethics of these two particular employees. What one of the salesmen did was to sell the product to a customer and then take it to a competing firm and tell that company that Jeremy was so busy he couldn't handle the work. In the process this saboteur salesman bragged that he was making more money than he knew what to do with because it was coming from two directions: his boss *and* the other company in which, for a price, he was secretly placing some of his orders. He was found out and summarily fired. The other salesman clandestinely took another job where he worked part-time simultaneously while supposedly working full time for and being paid generously by Jeremy. He also stole from his boss a new kind of product, which was Jeremy's financial mainstay, thus taking both a good idea as well as stealing some of Jeremy's customers in the process. He also plotted to take away three of Jeremy's other employees along with him when he made the full jump to the other company. This salesman, who was quite a thief, even stole copies of Jeremy's price book. Of course, this second salesman, when found out, was likewise fired. Ironically both of these devious, unethical, disloyal saboteurs were *very active* — not just ordinarily active, but *very active* in their respective churches even as all this underhanded and dishonest work was unfolding.

And what happened to Jeremy, the *good guy* in all this? The toll he paid for his subordinates' misbehavior was devastating! He literally stopped sleeping for months, and almost every night, sick in heart and body, he would rise just to walk around the house and often to vomit. My friend told me the psychological and emotional pain he suffered was the worst of all. He also took a big hit financially. Because of his good reputation, however, Jeremy recovered after some months, but he had to cut his prices in the process, and he had to work twelve hour days, seven days a week, just to survive. As my friend, Jeremy, was telling me this sad story across his dining room table one evening, he said he just couldn't believe that someone could be so cruel that he could do such things to another person. Don't you see how deadly sabotage can be? It is ruinous to the saboteur, but often and sadly sabotage takes a huge toll on the victim as well.

Sabotage also rears up its ugly head in the political arena. As a case in point, when the Civil War was eating the life out of Abraham Lincoln in 1864, this great President in our history had something else to contend with: *sabotage within his own cabinet.* Lincoln had as the Secretary of the Treasury, Salmon P. Chase, known as the handsomest man in the cabinet, who had had presidential aspirations all the way back to 1856 which then came to a head in 1864 as he again thirsted for the presidency and thus hoped to displace Lincoln to become the president himself. Wallowing in a cesspool of lies, Chase foolishly thought himself to be a better man than Lincoln. In the words of Nicolay and Hay, Lincoln's old friends from Springfield and then secretaries in the White House, Chase "held so poor an opinion of the President's intellect and character in comparison with his own, that he could not believe the people so blind as deliberately to prefer the President to himself." Still later these two friends and secretaries agreed as to Chase, that "there never was a man who found it so easy to delude himself." *Falling into the trap of self-deception: that is an essential component of sabotage!*

Put an oversized ego together with self-deception and then couple these two things together with a lust for power, and you have the formula for devious sabotage. According to Lincoln's bi-ographer, Carl Sandburg, "In scores of letters written to politicians, editors, ministers, Chase over a two-year period sought to spread the impression that in the midst of incompetents he was the one man who would know how if given the power." Along the way, this political saboteur mastered the art of speaking out of both sides of his mouth, sometimes seeming to support Lincoln but more often lamenting (according to someone's contemporary diary entry) "the President's want of energy and force, which he said paralyzed ev-erything. His weakness [is] crushing us." Even as Chase was sup-posed to be tending the Treasury in support of a major war, he was spending half his time nursing along his high political ambitions, thus draining away time and strength from his appointed responsi-bility. Lincoln was a mighty big man even to be able to put up with this as long as he did; even though in the end a humiliated Chase had to withdraw his candidacy and was forced to resign his cabinet position, Chase succeeded through his sabotage in making a lot of Republicans bitterly unhappy with President Lincoln and causing them to grumble on about his supposed crass ineptitude. People, there is pain here both in a bitterly disappointed Chase and in a heartbroken Lincoln, which is one of the things that makes the deadly sin of sabotage so *deadly*. More often than not, it cuts both ways.

Which brings us to the sorrowful example of the sabotage of our Lord Christ. As I write these words, it is Good Friday. This morning in my devotions I focused on the Cross on which our Savior, Jesus Christ, died for us. This afternoon I will go to our church where the congregation will ponder again the Seven Last Words of Jesus spoken even as his life was draining out of him. I can hear my Master say, "This I have done for you. What have you done for me?" If somehow I can douse the flames of some sabotage in this world and in the Church of Christ, the writing of this sermon will not be in vain.

Though Calvary was God's plan from the beginning, it still needs to be faced that there were many saboteurs along the way who, in effect, pounded the nails through the flesh of our Lord and Savior, Jesus Christ. From early on, according to John's Gospel, "... the Jews were looking for *a chance to kill him*" (John 7:1 NEB). I think we would all have to admit that in our lives we, too, have pounded some of those nails through the hands and feet of our Lord and thus sabotaged at least some of the things he was born into this world to do for us and for all humankind. Face the truth, folks! The most poignant way I know to put this is simply to quote a few of the verses in the New Testament — there are many more — that clearly illustrate how the deadly sin of sabotage led up to the crucifixion. Ponder anew the agony of the Cross as you hear these words, all of which occur in the Gospel narratives of Holy Week.

> *... the chief priests and the doctors of the law were trying* to devise some cunning plan *to seize him and put him to death.* (Mark 14:2 NEB)

> *Then the Pharisees went away and agreed on* a plan to trap him in his own words. (Matthew 22:15 NEB)

> *So they watched their opportunity and* sent secret agents *in the guise of honest men, to seize upon some word of his as a* pretext *for handing him over to the authority and jurisdiction of the Governor.* (Luke 20:22 NEB)

> *... they conferred together on a* scheme *to have Jesus arrested* by some trick *and put to death.* (Matthew 26:4 NEB)

> *... many came forward with* false evidence. (Matthew 26:59 NEB)

> *... the chief priests* stirred up the crowd *to have Pilate release Barabbas instead.* (Mark 15:11 NIV)

Need I go on? These are actually just a few of the verses, but were we so inclined, we could go on quoting verse after verse from all four Gospels, not only toward the end of Jesus' life, but throughout his ministry in which his enemies were, in a sly manner, continually turning their thoughts and efforts toward ridding themselves of Jesus of Nazareth. I suggest you notice this in your own Bible reading.

If, though you were blind to begin with, now you are able to see some sabotage all around ... if you are now able to acknowledge that sabotage is indeed deadly for both perpetrators and victims ... if you are willing to concede that the Bible has many examples of sabotage on its pages which you never noticed before ... if by looking around in life you notice perhaps for the first time how pervasive sabotage is in our society ... if you with sadness of heart are able to notice how sabotage threatens many an innocent person in a world like ours ... *then, certainly, you must know that sabotage has also invaded the precious Church of Jesus Christ.* So, therefore I invite you now to read on further into the next sermon which addresses this specific subject.

Sabotage In The Church

A Sermon Sorely Needed by Some Lay Persons and Some Clergy Persons; A Plea to Congregations to let the Holy Spirit Help them to Become more Christian; An Unpreached Sermon Written Especially for the Encouragement of Embattled Pastors

God be merciful to me, a sinner! (Luke 18:13b)

I, I am he who blots out your transgressions ... and I will not remember your sins. (Isaiah 43:25)

Repent, and believe in the good news. (Mark 1:15)

What we have been saying in the previous sermon is sad enough, to be sure, but when the poison of sabotage seeps into the Church of Christ it is especially sad and sometimes treacherous indeed. The first thing to do in solving any problem is to face the truth, and when we do that, it is true as Jesus said, "The truth will make you free" (John 8:32). The truth is that many among us are still crucifying the Lord Christ in and through his Church. The truth is that God is merciful and ever-ready to blot out all our transgressions. The truth is that He even is willing to remember our sins no more. The truth is that we need only repent of our sins including sabotage of the Church and believe in the good news of the gospel that Jesus came bringing.

Sabotage can happen, folks — *it can really happen in the Church!* — but first let's look at some facts, face some reality, and acknowledge the sad, sad truth that there is, in fact, the deadly sin of sabotage in the Church. Unfortunately, many people are still crucifying Christ in and through his Church. To illustrate this matter, I want to make two points on sabotage in the Church in our time, and I want to state these two points in such a penetrating way that I hope you will find them impossible to forget.

I

First, there are antagonists in the Church whose chief weapon is sabotage. These church members seem to make it their business to stir up trouble and dissension in the Church. Sometimes they do this subtly; sometimes they do it blatantly. Sometimes they do it under the guise of piety and high motivation; sometimes their Christian spirit is quite unattractive. As someone once wrote to me, "There certainly seems to be an evil spirit that's on the move within some of our church members." I suspect you all know what that means. Even though church sabotage is often done by someone piously claiming it is "for the good of the church," it is almost always done in a sub-Christian and often sneaky manner. The effect is inevitably the same: *trouble* and *dissension.*

Unfortunately — no! *sadly indeed!* — much sabotage in the Church stems from a power struggle. People, this ought not to be, but it is. And such is decidedly un-Christian! If you have trouble taking this from a clergyman, consider lay comments published in our church magazine, *The Lutheran.* One woman wrote, "The conflict I've seen is the result of two opposing groups of people — those who want the church to grow and those who want it to stay the same." A man wrote, "To be blunt, most conflicts are caused by emotionally ill people. Their need for power has led them to the Church ..." Another woman wrote, "The need for power is the most significant element in congregational conflict." I repeat, all this was written in our own Church magazine, *The Lutheran.*

So, such power-driven people who crave to control the congregation sharpen up such knives as they have and go to work. And what are these weapons? *They can make every issue "a federal case." They can see to it that nothing passes unanimously. They can impede real progress by practicing "terrorism" in committee and congregational meetings. They can massage any congregational statistics to spin these figures in such a way that they make things look bad. And then there is the ultimate weapon of sabotage: withdrawing a pledge (Either I get my way or I won't pay!).* I'm sure as I simply list these weapons of congregational saboteurs you know exactly what I mean and could cite many examples yourselves.

A church staff, too, can do much to undermine the authentic ministry of the Christian Church, and it, too, can become decidedly unchristian in nature. A dear woman and a splendid secretary as well once placed a letter on my desk informing me she would be looking for employment elsewhere. In part she wrote, "I want you to know that I truly love my job and all that is involved. I really like working for you, but find that I can no longer keep on working here with the situation like it is. I have never worked in a place where so much unlove, unkindness, and intolerance is shown toward one another. People try to get one another in trouble and go about spying on each other ... I cannot take this constant game playing of 'who is in control.'" This woman joined the staff as a "stranger" and an "outsider" and was thus undermined repeatedly by the "old timers" and the "church members of the staff" who had already been there a long time. It didn't seem to matter that this woman was more highly qualified and more competent than the others. That must have spawned no little jealousy. Moreover, it bothered them too, I think, that she was deeply loyal to her supervisor. Consequently, some of the staff members were just plainly out to get her. Shame on us whenever we let such as this happen to anyone in our midst without protest!

Sometimes in a church a single man can do considerable damage through his sabotage. Paul himself had that kind of trouble and named the perpetrator. The offender was Alexander the coppersmith. "Alexander the coppersmith did me great harm," wrote Paul in 2 Timothy, his last epistle. Then he went on to warn young Timothy, "You also must beware of him for he strongly opposed our message" (4:14-15). I personally have always appreciated such warnings from parishioners who truly love the Church. The enmity of Alexander against Paul — let's call him, *Saint Paul* for he was indeed a saint — seems to have been personal. One commentator suggested that Alexander may have been a secret enemy, a pretended disciple, who used his closeness to Paul to play the traitor, thus trying to entrap him. Greater than any personal pain Paul may have suffered, however, this saboteur "strongly opposed" the gospel message, not only thereby putting his very salvation in peril, but also and especially he thus held back the cause of Jesus Christ, that is, *the Church*. I have had "Alexanders" in every congregation I have served. Of one of them, another church member truthfully said, " 'Alexander' screws up everything he touches." I watched that happen, but that was not the worst of it. This man continuously undermined the forward progress of a great church. I confronted him, of course, but somebody else should have had the courage to stand boldly beside me in a matter of this importance and thus try to bring a screeching halt to his sabotage.

Moreover, sometimes in a church one woman can do considerable damage through her sabotage. There are "Jezebels" among us in church pews and alongside of us in church activities. One of the chief weapons of such women is *gossip*. As an outgrowth of this, they sometimes seem to hold the keys to secret and supposedly damaging information, which, of course, they never openly express because they can't, but the mere assumption that they have such damaging knowledge can in itself be quite subversive.

There is a vivid scene in a novel titled *Voice of the Eagle* by Linda Lay Shuler which has something to teach us here. A woman in the Indian tribe named Antelope and her family had been highly successful in bringing the tribe back from previous struggles and attacks from other tribes. Life then became better than it had ever been before in that Indian tribe as the leadership of this one family became both successful and effective as well as for the good of all. There was, however, a nagging undertow of constant untrue gossip regarding this powerful and effective family. People were pretty sure that one woman, Tookah, was the offender. None of the tribe, however, had the courage to face this formidable woman until one day Antelope, also known as "She Who Remembers," was in the right place at the right time. She boldly confronted this tribe gossip in a tribal meeting when, referring to Tookah, she said, "Obviously *we have a witch among us*, one who desires to harm me and my family by spreading venomous untruths." The popular Chief then forced Tookah to stand up. Trying meekly to defend herself, the tribe gossip said weakly and unconvincingly, "I have only the welfare of everyone in [the city] at heart. I meant no harm." Ever hear anything like that before? Then Tookah peered fiercely at Antelope and pointed a shaking finger at her and said, "I am *not* a witch!" To

100

which Antelope answered even more pointedly, "Then do not behave like one!" If the eyes of some congregational "Jezebel" falls on these words, think of what Jesus once said to a woman who had done no worse than Tookah: *"Go and sin no more!"*

Sometimes the ol' devil just gets into people. The only true cure for this is for the Holy Spirit to change such persons. One of the worst years of my life was 1965, and the one who primarily made it so later tried to apologize as best I suppose he could. He explained it this way, "I guess the ol' devil just got into me." Well, in our Christian freedom we do not have to acquiesce to that diabolic invasion of our souls. The Holy Spirit waits to strengthen us in the inner person as Scripture promises.

The remedy for all this is primarily for the laity to speak the truth in love, that is, to *confront* honestly in a Christian manner such troublemakers and saboteurs. In my second parish, I made a pastoral call on a man who, though friendly enough, told me frankly that the only way I could ever get him into the church building was feet first. When he later died, his wife initially suggested that he be buried from the church, but when I explained that actually he had so clearly rejected the church while living it would, therefore, be unfitting to hold the funeral service in the church and more appropriate to hold it in the funeral home. I told her that I would still give her husband the best funeral I knew how to give. The widow, who had some sense about her and remained my friend afterward, agreed. But then the funeral director, a member of the congregation, started to build up a firestorm of contention because I, a young pastor still wet behind the ears, had the audacity to refuse a church funeral for a good man. I've often wondered if the fact that the funeral director was a distant relative of the deceased could have had anything to do with that.

I'll never forget looking out the parsonage window that evening and seeing the vice president and secretary of the congregation walking together down the street from the town square toward the funeral home called, we suspected, by the funeral director. We braced ourselves for the worst. Instead they told that funeral director in no uncertain terms that they thought their pastor was right in this matter and that he should just keep quiet and serve only in the capacity of a funeral director rather than someone trying to bring disquiet to a peaceful congregation. A half-hour later these same two men marched right back to the parsonage and told my wife and myself exactly what had happened and what was said. The result: a congregational tumult was stopped dead in its tracks!

There is an epilogue to this true story. The widow, perhaps for the first time understanding the importance of church membership, herself professed faith in Christ as her Savior and joined the church. And several years later one of the deceased man's relatives even left the church a large bequest. Would that all congregational squabbles and brouhahas could be thus quietly and quickly stopped!

II

Second, there are those in the Church, including some who wear their collars backwards, whose sabotage is primarily an attack on the pastor. It is true, of course, that there are some pastors who are unworthy of this high calling. Such as these *should* be weeded out. We are *not* thinking here of this kind of unworthy pastor. Instead we are considering here capable, conscientious, Christian pastors called by Christ to serve in the Church. To be sure, sometimes even these good pastors need to be amenable to loving and loyal constructive criticism, and God bless those dear lay men and woman who know just how to do this with Christian dignity and with respect for their leader. My friends, there are many pastors who can and will profit by such appropriate criticism. When such pastors as these get a bit off the track, they are not too proud to make an appropriate course correction.

What frequently happens, however, is that it is precisely the *good pastors* who are under the most vicious attacks of sabotage. Somehow those who are eager to compromise and who don't ruffle any feathers with reality seem to escape most of this sabotage. At any rate, note that Christ himself, quoting the Old Testament, which he knew by heart, said to his disciples on the way to Gethsemane, "... it is written, 'I will strike the shepherd, and the sheep of the flock will be scattered' " (Matthew 26:31). It is my opinion, that this is the devil's usual way to attack and to hurt the Church in times like ours.

102

It is a curious and paradoxical fact of psychology that is so well documented that it is predictable that church members will often try to throw a pastor off — I'm quoting a famous psychologist now — "precisely when [those pastors] are functioning *at their best!*" Dr. Edwin H. Friedman continues, "This automatic, mindless sabotage of followers is so prevalent in human families [and institutions] that, if anything, *it is usually evidence that the leader has been functioning well.*" So, if a pastor is an effective leader, he is intimidating people. If he is leading the church in authentic Christian growth numerically and otherwise, some will say the church isn't like it used to be when it was more homey and small (when, of course, the old timers were running everything). If he is successfully capturing the attention of the congregation and the community through effective preaching, then preaching, after all, is not nearly as important as other aspects of church life. If he has achieved some reputation in the wider church and is therefore invited here and there to speak or make a witness, then he ought to stay home more and tend the flock. And so it goes. The attacks so often become most vicious when the called servant of God is functioning at his very best! To quote Dr. Friedman again, "Theories of leadership do not pay enough attention to the issue of sabotage, *the fact that* strength *is so scary to many....*"

As a corollary of this, a pastor who had wanted to become the senior pastor remaining on the staff of a congregation when the previous senior pastor retired or moved and then was passed over in favor of a "stranger from afar" can be especially devious, treacherous, and undermining. I could go on for a long while and give you illustrations of this from good pastors, whom I have come to know and love along the way in my more than 41 years of active ministry, who have almost literally had their hearts torn out of them because of the undertow of sabotage. Of all the places to test the character of a man or woman in the church and in the workaday world, to get so close to the front rank and then not quite make it, is a special place of testing. Many second pastors (associates or assistants) just don't have the spiritual maturity to make it to such high ground and thus *begin to pay back* for their disappointment by sabotaging the new senior pastor. I have seen that again and again throughout my years of service in Christ's Church, and so often the Synod is of little help in this situation. It takes maturity, on the part of a second pastor to affirm and respect the gifts and the call of the one placed over him or her by a call of God. (It should go without saying, of course, that the new senior pastor should also respect and affirm the gifts of the second pastor who works with him or her.) It takes deep humility for anyone to accept that God has other plans than that which we have tried to tell Him in our prayers. It takes authentic *big* Christianity to reach out in Christ-like love and genuine loyalty to the one called to sit where you had so badly wanted to sit.

So, sabotage ensues, albeit often unconsciously. Usually, it goes underground. The "weapons" of by-passed second pastors are well known in the profession: giving too much sympathetic hearing to malcontents, hugging protectively one's turf and portfolio lest the new senior pastor share more fully in the ministry of the congregation, undermining the work of the church with criticism disguised as humor, developing a clandestine following of "groupies" to listen to their whining and to bolster their egos, being silent when he or she ought to speak up for the right and the true, cultivating and encouraging a congregational cold shoulder toward the man or woman who has been properly called to be the leader, and whenever possible in congregational issues just letting the new senior pastor twist in the wind. Need I go on? It is better for the King's business that such a disgruntled clergyperson take a call elsewhere.

The sad result of all this is that often the senior pastor is denied the psychological leadership of the congregation and thus can *do no great works*. The result is that if the senior pastor is a good man and really cares, in order to save the congregation from schism, he must "work like sixty" and spend an inordinate amount of time keeping "chaos on a leash." The result is that the senior pastor, who *could* lead the congregation splendidly forward, must instead be compelled just to "grind out yardage" slowly toward whatever worthy goals that have been set. The result may well be that the senior pastor cannot sleep at night and thus is unable to work effectively during the day further fueling whatever "fire" there may be that he is just not up to the job. The result may actually be that the health of the senior pastor breaks. The result is that the senior pastor may grow so discouraged in well-doing that he may seek another call or just retire early, thus preventing his gifts from being used to the utmost by the Highest. All such things are sad and even heartbreaking. But don't forget the root of all this is almost inevitably the deadly sin of sabotage by the other pastor or pastors who should really know better and care more deeply for the overall spiritual health of the congregation.

Not infrequently the perpetrator of sabotage is perceived to be quite holy and Christian. This is especially true in the case of an ex-pastor, probably to keep his ego intact and flying high, stays around the congregation after retirement and thus rather automatically becomes a symbol of any "golden age," real or imaginary, which once *might* have been. Sometimes the ex-pastor doesn't even need to say much or do anything. Just *being there* drains off loyalty which should be rightly transferred to the new pastor who has been duly called by the congregation.

One of my friends published posthumously a book written out in longhand by his saintly father shortly before his death. Both father and son are now deceased, but I am proud to say that I knew them personally from early on in my ministry. Before my elderly clergy friend succeeded his predecessor senior pastor way back in 1943, a man whom he genuinely respected and appreciated for many things and toward whom he was always gracious and courteous, he could, nevertheless, write these words a half-century later of that predecessor simply because they were true.

> *He took no genuine interest in the church program or its organization ... He had not changed in thirty years. Our run-down and obsolete church building was "good enough" for him. When I finally established the church office, he brought the secretary a book to read in her spare time. (Note: this was already a large congregation.) I was continually frustrated ... At his last church council meeting, he pulled out a motion which he read to the council. The motion was to the effect that nothing was to be changed in the church in any way during my ministry.*

How can any successor do his best work under such a cloud? As though this were not enough for the new senior pastor to contend with, however, there was also a building program in the offing. That congregation was still growing and had a great future numerically, to say nothing of the service opportunities readily available in the community. At the same time this sizeable church was frustrated by being housed in an old building that was no longer adequate. Quite naturally, there was serious talk in the congregation of raising money, contracting with an architect, and building a new church adequate for the booming post World War II era. The successor, being a polite and gracious man and hoping against hope for some support from his predecessor in such a project, invited the old man to say a few words one Sunday to the worshiping congregations. Whereupon this elderly former senior pastor stood up in church, and this is what he said: "This a beautiful auditorium. It was good enough for me for 43 years. I don't know why it is not good enough for [name of successor]." That was enough to kill the building program for ten years!

Eventually, though, that church was built. It was dedicated in 1956. I have seen the beautiful colonial sanctuary which still stands so majestically in that city and still points its spire meaningfully toward Heaven. It is an awe inspiring building with a very worshipful sanctuary, but it should have been built long before it was.

It makes good sense, I think, for a retired pastor to move his membership elsewhere lest he, even though well-intentioned and saintly, indulge in the deadly sin of sabotage, perhaps just by *being there* and siphoning off the love and loyalty which could and should, to the glory of God, be transferred to the new pastor.

The net result of all this sabotage in the church is that the Church of Jesus Christ is seriously thwarted and held back. The power of Christ is short-circuited. We read of Jesus in the Bible that in his hometown of Nazareth, "He did not do many deeds of power there, because of their unbelief" (Matthew 13:58). What a pity! What might have been *wasn't* because of their unbelief, their non-receptiveness, their lack of humility, their unwillingness to grow. Many a church has likewise been greatly hindered because of the deadly sin of sabotage. And it is the gospel message that suffers.

106

A friend of mine, Russell C. Lee, wrote a book out of his long pastoral experience in which he gave his readers much spiritual meat upon which to chew. I copied down these words which, I believe, suggest a good remedy that could prevent much sabotage of pastors *by* pastors or lay persons. I have this quote on one of my 3 x 5 cards which I have collected over the years and which have so influenced my faith and life as a human being and as a Christian. Consider this, all ye who are prone to sabotage: "... people with a high sense of self-regard are humble, yet confident. They are able to affirm themselves, respect themselves, value themselves in such a way that *enables them to affirm, respect and value other people.*" And here, too, is something toward which we all might aspire which is the perfect antidote for sabotage. Long ago I copied these words on another of my valuable 3 x 5 cards: "The better we feel about ourselves, the fewer times we have to knock somebody else down to feel tall."

Where, then, does all this leave us? I invite you to return to where we started with a text I hope you understand even more deeply than before: "One thing I do know, that though I was blind, *now I see*" (John 9:25). I ask you also to think reflectively about this expanded version of the publican's prayer: " 'God be merciful to me, a sinner,' for *I, too, have sometimes been guilty of the deadly sin of sabotage.*" I urge you finally to contemplate seriously some words spoken by our Lord on Good Friday which now apply to others with whom we must now continue to work: *"Father, forgive them; for they know not what they do"* (Luke 23:34).

Manger Power Unleashed

A Christmas Eve Sermon

Our Saviour Lutheran Church
Christiansburg, Virginia
December 24, 1998

Max Lucado has written a book with the interesting title, *No Wonder They Call Him the Savior.* We easily recall on Christmas Eve that the angel said to the shepherds, "Unto you is born this day in the city of David a *Savior* ..." (KJV). Later Saint Paul wrote that in this Jesus "dwelleth all the fullness of the Godhead bodily" (KJV). But ever before these things were spoken, an angel told Joseph that the baby in Mary's womb was to be named "Jesus, for he will save his people from their sins." and that He would also be known as "Emmanuel, which means, 'God with us' " (RSV). My point is that once unleashed the world has never been able to stop the saving power of the Christ Child, for his power is of God. Thus, *No Wonder They Call Him the Savior.*

Now for a bit of humor at my expense which might even give you a hook by which to remember this sermon. In 1971 a parishioner told me something I just couldn't believe — namely, that one cannot break an egg with one's bare hand. Knowing, I thought, that an egg shell is a very fragile thing, I set out to prove that person wrong. I took an egg in my right hand, put my hand down deep into a laundry tub, and then squeezed it with all my might. To my utter amazement, I could not break it. Later I tried this experiment several more times, and not once was I able to crush an egg with my bare hand.

I found a children's sermon in this for Christmas Eve, 1971. I was going to point out that what I simply could not do with my 200 pounds, a little chicken weighing only a few ounces could do by pecking its way out. There seemed to be a hidden power in a little chicken's beak which a grown man's hand could not equal. I was going to use this as an illustration of the fact that the world itself could not stop the Christ Child wrapped in swaddling clothes and lying in a manger.

Unfortunately and disastrously, I tried the experiment one final time. In my office that Christmas Eve, with my vestments on, my sermon manuscript on the desk, and with some friends in the office, I tried once more with all my might to crush an egg with my hand. And this time the egg shattered all over the place: on my desk, on my sermon manuscript, on my ministerial vestments, on the wall across the room, and on the good clothes of our guests. I don't yet understand what happened though I strongly suspect there was a small unseen crack in that particular egg or some inherent weakness. I don't suggest any of you try this, but I am still convinced that a human hand cannot break a healthy egg. That Christmas Eve I had to give that children's sermon without my prop, of course, but my point, I believe, still stands — namely, that what a human being is not strong enough to do, a little almost helpless chicken can do and thus enter the world.

My point then and now is this: there is infinite saving power in the Holy Child of Bethlehem — let's call it manger-power — infinite saving power which this world has never been able to stop. So we can appropriately say, *No Wonder They Call Him the Savior!* Let me illustrate.

Consider Herod the Great who was made King of the Jews by the Roman Senate in 40 B.C. and ruled for 36 years. This man had the audacity to think he could wipe out God's Anointed by killing the innocents of Bethlehem. Herod had ascended to his position of power in the usual ways with political shrewdness, Oriental cunning, diplomatic skill, and military astuteness. He had held his power with an unprincipled reign of terror. He had initiated a worldly kingdom so grandiose that even the kingdoms of David and Solomon paled by comparison. Some of the ruins of Herod's kingdom can still be seen in our time. Furthermore, there is no way around the fact that Herod was a man of exceptional ability. Some say he was the greatest king of the day. They didn't call this ol' boy "Herod the Great" for nothing. And yet, the power of God in that Holy Infant cradled in a manger was infinitely greater, for Joseph, forewarned

110

by God in a dream, carried away the Baby Jesus to the safety of Egypt, thus avoiding the slaughter of the innocents in Bethlehem intended to kill the Newborn King. Moreover, we wouldn't even know who Herod was were it not for the Babe of Bethlehem.

Jesus, quite in contrast to Herod, had no aspirations of building a worldly kingdom. He had a chance, you will remember, when the devil in the wilderness offered him "all the kingdoms of the world and their splendor," but our Lord soundly rejected this offer. With consistency Jesus never compromised the spiritual manifestations of the Kingdom of God he preached. In the beginning of his ministry Jesus said, "The time is fulfilled, and the kingdom of God has come near; repent, and believe in the good news." At the end of his ministry when asked by Pilate, "Are you the King of the Jews?" Jesus replied, "My kingship is not of this world" (RSV). So they took him away and crucified him. In succinct words, the Apostles' Creed states, "He ... was crucified, died, and was buried." But this was by no means the end of the man from Nazareth. He so loved his friends and even his enemies that his love would not let them go. Therefore, *No Wonder They Call Him the Savior!*

The Creed continues, "On the third day he rose again." Peter said in his Pentecost sermon: "God raised him up, having freed him from death, because" — hear this well: *"because it was impossible for him to be held in [death's] power"* (Acts 2:24). One of the most dramatic portrayals I know of the resurrection triumph occurs in Dorothy Sayer's twelfth play on the life of Jesus titled, "The King Comes to His Own." Dorothy Sayers was a British writer of mysteries, but she also wrote a classic series of twelve plays on the life of Christ which were widely broadcast on the radio. Listen to Sequence 2, Act I of her final play which dramatically introduces the irresistible power of the resurrection:

> *The cocks begin to crow. Then the sound of three heavy earthquake shocks. Next, from a distance, the feet of men running in disorder. They draw near and die away. Then a heavy knocking, repeated with haste and urgency; and a frightened voice crying, "My Lord Caiaphas! My Lord Caiaphas!"*

It was *impossible,* you see, for Christ to be held by the power of death! *No Wonder They Call Him the Savior!*

Furthermore, through all the centuries, the gospel message of God's love and power could not be stopped. It was given to the Church to proclaim and to share, for Christ said, "You will be my witnesses" (Acts 1:8). He also said, "Upon this rock" — meaning faith in himself as Lord and Savior — "Upon this rock I will build my Church; and the gates of hell shall not prevail against it" (Matthew 16:18 KJV). The early Christians, so imbued with the power of the resurrection, were able to outlive and outdie all their adversaries and persecutors. As a matter of historical fact, the Church of Jesus Christ spread like a prairie fire across the ancient world until it actually threatened the pomp and power of Rome itself. As the persecutions against the Christians heated up, the cry became, "The Christians to the lions." There was something of a panic in that outcry!

This fierce struggle is what the book of Revelation is about. I was teaching a series of Bible studies on this last book of the Bible when one of my students came up asking that a friend of hers might be invited to the next class. This friend, so she said, had actually discovered in Revelation a passage that predicted the rise that had only recently taken place in the price of hamburger. Nonsense! The book of Revelation has nothing to do with the price of hamburger. As you are able to see through the symbolism which makes this book so difficult to understand, Revelation is about — I'm quoting James Stewart the Scottish divine now — Revelation is about "the Rome of the Caesars and the Church of the Galilean locked in the death-grapple." Dr. Stewart further describes the backdrop of Revelation in these words: "the second Babylon (the code word for Rome) — the second Babylon, mother of all the abominations of the earth, drunk with the blood of the friends of Jesus, laughing in the intoxication of her triumph, shrieking with laughter to see the poor, pathetic Body of Christ being crushed and mangled and battered out of existence." Against this background, John takes up his pen to write. And what does he write? Does he write, Rome is too much for us? Run for your lives? All is lost? Not that, but this: "Fallen, fallen is Babylon the great!" (14:8). Rome is done for, he

112

was saying. John knew the eternal, all-powerful God would have the last word. So with the ring of iron in it, John could write, "The kingdom of the world has become the kingdom of our Lord and of his Christ, and he will reign for ever and ever" (11:15 RSV). No! Revelation has nothing to do with the price of hamburger. It has everything to do with the power of Almighty God in Christ Jesus. If you want to know the gist of this Christ-centered book in a single verse, here it is in the nineteenth chapter, the sixth verse: "Alleluia: for the Lord God omnipotent reigneth" (KJV). Remember that throbbing theme: "... the Lord God omnipotent *reigneth*!" Everything in this last book of the Bible hinges on these triumphant words!

"Unto you is born this day in the city of David a Saviour" — a *Savior* — "which is Christ the Lord" (Luke 2:11 KJV). The miracle of the Christmas gospel is that the saving grace of the Lord Jesus Christ released into the world has meant salvation for humankind for nearly 2,000 years. Mark this: the salvation of God let loose in Bethlehem long ago comes even yet with power and might into our generation.

Some of us here are old enough to remember that "day of infamy" in 1941 when the Japanese bombers surprised Pearl Harbor, killing and wreaking havoc. What a day! Who can put into words the outrage we Americans felt at this infamous attack. I was a ninth grader at the time, but I remember well my own fury at the attack as our principal gathered us in the gym the next day to hear President Roosevelt's address to Congress which then declared war. Even if you were not yet born by then, you know, of course, about that December seventh attack from your study of history. But I wonder if you also know that which the history books do not tell — namely, that the pilot who led that deceitful and treacherous attack, Captain Mitsuo Fuchida, later became a Christian? Feeling that irresistible love that would not let him go, the power of God proved to be too much for him. And so he surrendered his life to Jesus Christ as Lord and Savior. But there is more: In the early fifties this Japanese bomber pilot came to the United States, studied in a seminary in this country, and then went back to Japan as a Christian missionary. Incredible, you think! Yes, but this kind of spiritual miracle has made Christian history for 2,000 years. *No Wonder They Call Him the Savior!*

The world has never been able to stop the Christian gospel, but what the world cannot do, you and I in our God-given freedom can do. "Behold, I stand at the door and knock" (Revelation 3:20 RSV) says the Lord, but you and I can keep that door into our lives *closed*! And yet, after all these years since the first Christmas, it is still profoundly true that, "Where meek souls will receive him, still, the dear Christ enters in."

Confessions Of A Troubled Soul

A Dramatic Monologue Sermon for Palm Sunday

Our Saviour Lutheran Church
Christiansburg, Virginia
April 16, 2000

It is a sobering experience to be *struck* with the bitter realiza-
tion of what you might have been but failed to be in a crucial hour.
You see, at a decisive moment, *I let a pivotal chance pass me by.* I
should have put my life and reputation on the line. I should have
protested vehemently to that high Jewish council, "This is an outrage! You are planning to murder God's Messiah!" *But I did not do
that.* I was silent when my words could have counted. I learned
later that Jesus had said, "Those who are ashamed of me and my
words ... of them the Son of Man will also be ashamed when he
comes in his glory...." I tried to rationalize my failure to speak up,
but all the while I knew what was right and I knew what they were
planning to do him was cruelly wrong. So all history knows me
now as Nicodemus who, for fear of the Jews, was a secret disciple.

But you, sitting nonchalantly in your pew, you, too, know the
difference between right and wrong. Furthermore, you know now
that Jesus Christ is the Savior of the world and that he rose from
the dead and lives and reigns in all eternity. For all that, you often
do nothing or say nothing while evil rages, and again and again
you fail to speak up for Christ. You are timid when you should be
brave, quiet when you should be outspoken. Shame on you! Shame
on me, too!

My great chance to stand up for the truth has come and gone,
but you still have many chances when you can be his defender and
his representative in your wild generation. To stand up for Jesus
may bring ridicule and unpopularity; it may bring difficulty and
sacrifice. But remember, Jesus said, "Whoever denies me before
others, I also will deny before my Father in Heaven." Perhaps this

115

day if you can come to know how I failed and how I might have been a disciple in the open, then you will be ready for your great hour of testing as I was not. For the sake of the Christ you have come here to worship; I ask you, please, to give me a hearing as I begin now at the beginning.

John's Gospel tells you I was "a leader of the Jews." This meant that I was a member of the party of the Pharisees. Now some of the Pharisees made much ado about exceedingly small points of the Law, but for the most part, we studied and taught and practiced the Holy Law of God. This had been revealed to us in the sacred writings. Our "delight [was] in the Law of the Lord." Not only was I a Pharisee, but I was also a member of that prestigious Jewish body known as the Sanhedrin. This elite body, you might say, was the highest legislative, judicial, and executive body of the Jewish nation. *It was supposed to act for the good of our people.* But throughout what you know as the passion drama, the Sanhedrin did not do any good and, in fact, behaved badly. I saw all this from the *inside* from whence I am now telling my story as, I suspect, you have never heard it before.

One of the Sanhedrin's duties was to deal with those suspected of being false prophets. In those days there were wild and rabid leaders teaching doctrines dangerous to the Judaism we cherished. It was routine, therefore, that Caiaphas, our high priest, should assign spies to report upon a certain Galilean carpenter whose upstart teaching and disregard for ecclesiastical authority alarmed us. It was even said that he performed miracles. Over a period of months the reports upon his strange ways and curious words became a regular part of our agenda. We became worried and uneasy over the growing size of his following. Moreover, he utterly confounded our spies with his answers to their questions. Our spies were experienced men. They were schooled in asking loaded questions, but this Jesus always had an answer that threw them back on their heels. When they returned to tell the Sanhedrin about their conversations with this Jesus of Nazareth, I sometimes found myself laughing on the inside but, of course, never on the outside in that august body. Jesus was entirely too masterful for them to handle even though they were well-versed in our religion and Scripture. Naturally, these things made the Sanhedrin resent Jesus; but strangely enough I found myself becoming more and more fascinated with him. At that time it even occasionally flickered across my mind that he just might be the long-awaited Messiah, but I never once discussed my feelings with any of the other members. I just found myself being fascinated and, perhaps more importantly, *strangely drawn to him.*

After some months of hearing reports of Jesus' teaching and miracles, I heard that he was in Jerusalem for the Passover Feast. I wanted to hear him teach and perhaps see a miracle, but it would never do for a member of the exalted Sanhedrin to go listen to him without heckling him. I couldn't do that. It didn't seem right. I therefore decided to seek him out "by night" as your Scriptures tell you. I went to ask questions that were bothering me. I admit that I went under cover of darkness because I was afraid. But there was another reason. I really wanted a private conversation with Jesus which would have been impossible in the daytime. You might also say that I came in the darkness because I needed light.

He received me cordially, but in his first sentence he seized the initiative, saying, "Very truly, I tell you, no one can see the kingdom of God without being born from above." It was as though he were saying to me throughout this conversation, *"Nicodemus, if you're really interested in what I am doing, you might as well know from the beginning that you've got to start from scratch. You think you belong to the kingdom of God, but that is not a matter of rules and regulations; it is a matter of attitude and disposition. Your pride in law-keeping has to move over and give way to a humble trust in God for salvation."* He was talking about a kind of change that changes everything. He was speaking of life under new management. Such rebirth, he was saying, must come from above and be of the Spirit. It had to be a total about-face regarding religion. No longer was religion to be about doing things to court God's favor. Rather, religion was to be about receiving God in your hearts. Such was like being born all over again. We talked from midnight to dawn on these important spiritual matters, and I will never forget the memorable words from which he left me. He said, "For God so loved the world that He gave His only Son, so that everyone who believes in him may not perish but may have eternal life." That

117

sentence kept coming back to me through all that followed. When I left Jesus that early morning, I was sure of one thing: He was not the crackpot my colleagues thought he was.

Months passed. During this time, with Jesus as my teacher, I did more thinking about religion than I had ever done before. Our spies, you see, kept us well informed of what Jesus was saying to the people and also what he was doing. All the while, I said nothing, unfortunately, though I was still quite impressed with him, especially when I remembered what he had said to me in our nighttime conversation. Almost without realizing what was happening, I built up a great deal of sympathy for him. In the hostile discussions we were having in the Sanhedrin about this Galilean, I found myself secretly and silently siding with Jesus. At the time I thought I was the only one growing to respect him. Later I learned that he had another secret disciple in our midst. It was Joseph of Arimathea.

At last, my cautious and timid support broke into words. This happened when Jesus was once again in Jerusalem, this time for the Feast of the Tabernacles. Over my unspoken protest the Sanhedrin sent the Temple police to arrest Jesus for questioning. They returned empty-handed, saying, "Never has anyone spoken like this!" I was amused. The chief priests and scribes just couldn't handle him. He was too much for them. Anyway, Caiaphas, who was supposedly a "holy man," went right ahead passing judgment on Jesus, which was clearly in conflict with our Law. It was at this meeting for the only time that I mustered up enough courage to say anything. I pointed out from Scripture how the Sanhedrin was in violation of our own procedures of justice. I was quickly put down! They said to me sarcastically, "Surely you are not also from Galilee, are you? Search and you will see that no prophet is to arise from Galilee." That was an irrelevant non-answer; it had nothing to do with what I had said. But it was enough to intimidate me into a silence that was not to be broken in the more crucial meetings that followed.

A few more months passed, and then to everybody's amazement, Jesus actually raised a man named Lazarus from the dead. The fact of this miracle was undeniable. Everybody knew it had taken place. Our own spies had actually seen it happen. Well, this dead man, Lazarus, made alive again so threatened the Jewish religion that the chief priests even suggested that we kill the poor man again. Anyway, after this miracle Caiaphas hastily called another meeting of the Sanhedrin. That was the only time I ever saw our holy leader a bit unnerved and edgy. Caiaphas lashed out against Jesus, spewing out hostile venom in his words. I should have protested, but, shamefully, I said nothing. The high priest, however, was at no loss for words. Sizing up the situation, he said to that holy body with a snarl in his voice, "You know nothing at all!" That was insulting. We weren't stupid. We were among the brightest and best of Judaism. "You are nothing at all!" he sneered. *"You do not understand that it is better for you to have one man die for the people than to have the whole nation destroyed."* In saying that, of course, the high priest was afraid that our nation would be crushed under the heel of Rome because of this, which is something that happened anyway in 70 A.D. Caiaphas could not have known and never even realized later that his words were actually true and prophetic but in a way he never intended. Truly, one Man was to die for the people, *the Lamb of God who takes away the sin of the world*! At any rate, when Caiaphas said what he said, Jesus was doomed to die. His words were a death warrant, but I, Nicodemus, just sat there *scared silent.*

The next thing I knew Jesus was entering the Holy City like a king. He entered Jerusalem triumphantly on that day you call Palm Sunday. It seemed as though the whole world had gone after him as people by the thousands threw palm branches in his path and shouted loudly, "Hosanna to the Son of David! Blessed be he who comes in the name of the Lord! Hosanna in the highest." This was clearly messianic, which was enough to throw the Sanhedrin into near-panic. I saw! I heard! And I prayed, "My God! What is all this coming to?"

You moderns should be able to understand how I felt. You have seen many times the tragic motion pictures which show vividly the assassination of your President Kennedy. Surely you have thought while seeing these pictures, "Stop it! This can't be happening!" But it did happen, and nothing stopped it. That first Palm Sunday I saw that Jesus was on a collision course with my own Sanhedrin.

119

They were out to kill him. I know now that I could not have stopped the crucifixion. *I know now it was God's plan of salvation.* But I did not know that then.

When I might have said something in behalf of Jesus, however, I did not do it. I did not defend God's Messiah. I spoke not a single word of protest against their cruel and deadly plot to crucify him. Shame on me! But shame on you, too, for the many chances you have let go right on by you to speak up for your Lord and Savior Jesus Christ. *O shame, thrice shame upon us all.*

Despite all this, I want you to know, *there is still hope!* There is hope for you *now* even as there was hope for me *then.* After Calvary, you see, came Easter! When I saw the love of God streaming down from the Cross and then experienced the reality of the resurrection, I became a believer and a disciple. What happened to me was the same as being born all over again, just as Jesus had said. And if this could happen to me, a cowardly secret disciple, it can happen to *anyone! Even when we fail — thank God! — there is still the hope of redemption.* Come along with me next Sunday, therefore, as we go together all the way through the passion drama to its triumphant culmination: *the glorious victory of Easter.*

A Voice From The Inside Of The Sanhedrin

A Dramatic Monologue Sermon for Easter Sunday

Our Saviour Lutheran Church
Christiansburg, Virginia
April 23, 2000

A week ago on Palm Sunday when we last met here in this
sanctuary, I, Nicodemus, confessed to you my shame at being a
secret disciple of Jesus for fear of the Jews. I also shared with you
my nighttime visit with Jesus and explained how he had spoken to
me of being born again. I further told you of the one and only time
I did rather timidly speak up in Jesus' behalf before the Sanhedrin
only to be quickly put down. Then, following the raising of Lazarus,
I recalled for you how Caiaphas, our unholy high priest, stated
ominously, "You do not understand that it is better for you to have
one man die for the people than to have a whole nation destroyed."
That was the same thing as signing a death warrant on Jesus. At
that significant meeting, when I might have courageously risen to
Jesus' defense, I was instead *scared silent*. Then after that messianic outpouring of acclaim and wild Hosannas on Palm Sunday,
Caiaphas, our high priest, became even more obsessed with doing
Jesus into death.

The week that followed, which you moderns call "Holy Week,"
I was to get no rest at all. For one thing, it is not easy on the ner-
vous system of a human being to keep the right bottled up on the
inside. The other thing was that we had almost continuous meetings of the Sanhedrin to hear reports of what Jesus was saying and
doing. I must tell you, by this time my heart, if not my voice, was
calling him "Lord and Master!" We learned that week that he drove
the merchants and the moneychangers right out of the Temple, saying, "My house shall be called a house of prayer; but you are making it a den of robbers." I thought, *Someone should have said that
a long time ago!* Then he told three parables that any fool could see

121

were bold expositions of the unfruitfulness of Israel. I thought, *He is so right!* He turned the tables on some of our scheming leaders who were trying to entrap him regarding the Roman tax, saying, "Give therefore to the emperor the things that are the emperor's, and to God the things that are God's." I thought, *He makes so much sense! How can they miss it?* He pronounced woe upon the Scribes and Pharisees, calling us "hypocrites." I thought, *We are hypocrites, and better sooner than later, we should face up to it!* He even predicted the destruction of Herod's magnificent Temple, saying, "I tell you, not one stone will be left here upon another; all will be thrown down." I thought, *Why not? The Spirit of the Lord has already departed from this place!* These were all dangerous things for him to say and do. I wanted to rush out and warn him of the perilous path he was following, but, of course, that is something secret disciples don't dare do. As that sleepless week wore on, it was dreadfully obvious that Caiaphas, our chief holy man, like a venomous snake, was just waiting to strike the death blow.

Inevitably the final clash between Jesus and the Sanhedrin came. It came at a hastily called meeting about midnight on Thursday. I think you should know, dear people, that it was downright illegal for the Sanhedrin to meet at night, but meet we did. And what a travesty of justice was perpetrated that awful night! Caiaphas ran roughshod over our own well-prescribed laws, obsessed as he was. And do you know what that crafty and diabolic Caiaphas had done? He had actually bribed one of Jesus' own disciples to betray him for thirty miserable pieces of silver. That's the kind of spiritual leader we had leading our nation headlong into destruction. Moreover, he had hired some professional witnesses to testify against Jesus, but they were so inept that they couldn't even get their well-rehearsed stories straight. In the end their testimony was thrown out. Still, Jesus of Nazareth, who stood magnificently before us, was convicted and sentenced to death. At least a dozen regulations of our own Jewish Law stood between Jesus and a death sentence, but they were all shunted aside or ignored in this mad attempt to put Jesus out of the way once and for all. We had safeguards built into our legal system to make it impossible to convict an innocent man, but this highest of Jewish courts, which above all should have known better, was insanely blinded with irrational hatred. *And all the while I, Nicodemus, a shameful secret disciple, sat there and said not a word!* I could see they were actually fighting God. *But still I said nothing!*

I was so terribly ashamed that all I could do after that horrendous meeting was to slink out into the darkness, go to my home, and drench my pillow with tears. While I berated myself and wept through the night, Caiaphas tangled with Pilate. He was much too clever for that Roman Governor, and before he was finished twisting him around his finger, as I learned later, Pilate finally gave in and "... handed [Jesus] over to them to be crucified." So it was that early on that Friday you call Good, the Roman soldiers took an Innocent Man carrying his own cross and paraded him on the Via Dolorosa through Jerusalem to a skull-shaped hill named Golgotha.

"There they crucified him, and with him two others, one on either side, with Jesus between them." I was too scared to be there, of course, but in bits and pieces as the day struggled along, I heard what was happening. I heard how he calmly received the nails through his flesh without so much as a whimper. I heard that he looked down from the cross at his persecutors who had brought him there and pounded the nails and said, "Father, forgive them; for they do not know what they are doing." I heard that the chief priest and his cohorts climbed that hill to scoff at him and that disgusted me. I heard that as darkness clouded the sky even as the life was ebbing out of him, he died with a prayer on his lips, saying, "Father, into your hands I commend my spirit." They even told me that the Roman centurion, recognizing his innocence, seeing his composure, and admiring his courage, exclaimed in the end, "Truly this man was God's Son!"

These things I heard; they rest I saw and felt. I saw for myself the "darkness (which) came over the whole land ... while the sun's light failed." I felt for myself the very earth shake beneath me as he died. I later even saw with my own eyes "the curtain of the temple [which was as thick as a man's hand that had been] torn in two, from top to bottom" as though some giant hands had ripped it asunder. Although it was as though God were saying with all the power of nature, "This is my beloved Son, with whom I am well pleased."

123

Enveloped in a cloud of grief resulting from this tragic day, I scarcely could hear a knocking at my door. It went on a while before I was startled into responding. It was "Joseph of Arimathea, a respected member of the [Sanhedrin] who," I learned, "was also himself waiting expectantly for the Kingdom of God." All along, he told me, he had sensed a secret and unspoken camaraderie between us in looking for the Kingdom of God. With no little courage, Joseph had already sought and received permission from Pilate to bury the body of Jesus in his own "new tomb in which no one had ever been laid." Joseph asked me to join him in burying Jesus, and since by then I had become tired to the core of cowardly secret discipleship, I was ready and even anxious to be of assistance. I brought the necessary myrrh and aloes. Joseph had the linen cloths. We walked as fast as we could to the hill where they had crucified him. We took the body down as reverently and gently as we could. We then carried it to the garden and buried him there as was the burial custom of the Jews. The last thing we did was to roll a stone against the door of the tomb and seal it. What we did, kind and even a bit brave as it was, seemed to be too little, too late.

Nothing — *nothing whatsoever* — could have prepared me for what happened next! Before dawn on the first day of the week there came a frantic knocking at my door. A runner had come with a call to still another meeting of that accursed Sanhedrin of which by now I was ashamed of being a member. I thought, "What now?" I dragged heavy feet to that meeting with my mind cluttered with profoundly negative thoughts only to hear the most amazing tidings of good news imaginable. *Jesus had actually risen from the dead!* In a flash of insight, I *knew for sure that he was the long-awaited Messiah!* I could also say from the depths of my soul that which you have sung today, *"I know that my Redeemer lives!"*

At this meeting, I couldn't keep from laughing out loud. It was pathetic as well as funny how those guards were trying to tell what had happened in the Easter Garden. They stammered and stuttered and shook as they explained the quaking earth beneath their feet, as they told of an unearthly creature rolling away the stone, as they described how this creature's "appearance was like lightning, and his clothing white as snow." I kid you not, people, those proud and brave Roman soldiers were actually quaking in fear before us. Instead of

124

staying to investigate this strange happening, they had scampered back to Caiaphas, hoping, I suppose, for some kind of protection against Caesar. Even Caiaphas was visibly shaken at their report, but my heart was singing, "Hallelujah!" With customary underhandedness, however, Caiaphas bribed the guards to tell a deliberate lie. "You must say," he told them, "his disciples came by night and stole him away while we were asleep." It was a ridiculous excuse, and the only thing that made it possibly workable was that Caiaphas promised if this resurrection during their watch reached Pilate's ears that he, the high priest, would somehow keep them out of trouble. What a day that was! What a day to *remember* and *celebrate*!

Perhaps by now you can guess what happened next? Then and there I stopped being a secret disciple. My cowardly mouth was unstopped. The rest of the Sanhedrin found themselves speechless at this early morning meeting, but not I. While they sat in stunned silence, I resigned! Then, with the intensity of a laser beam that went right through them, I said,

> *I have no wish to serve another minute in a body so devoid of principle, so manipulative for their own selfish purposes, so far along on the road to ruin that dissolution and destruction are now inevitable. You are no better than the blind who try to lead the blind. And I have no respect whatsoever for the one among us who calls himself the high priest and then contrives and lies and distorts the truth in such a way that God's Messiah is nailed to a cruel cross. Moreover, I have done some reading in our Scriptures as you with your political agenda have had too little time to do. Isaiah the prophet and the others predicted what has happened during these days. It was also foretold that a new movement of the faithful remnant, which Jesus called the "Church," would arise and carry on the mission committed to us which Israel has so disastrously failed to do.*

When I finished my speech of resignation, there was a spontaneous gasp erupting from the 68 remaining men on that now, impotent Jewish Body. Then and there I walked out, never to return.

Friends, after that my whole life was changed, inside and outside! *The Risen Christ gave me new birth from above and by the Holy Spirit.* Praise God! Furthermore, *Jesus Christ captured my wholehearted allegiance.* This was to be easier than halfhearted devotion. *Still further, I and his followers became exhilaratingly alive.* Ours became **LIFE**, you might say, in capital letters and bold-faced type! And how did all this happen? For me, it happened because *"I (knew) the One in whom I (had) put my trust ..." He was indeed the Master and Lord of Life!*

Not only was I privileged to see the Risen Christ, a privilege not given to the Sanhedrin, I saw how God was speaking the last and greatest word. I heard with my own ears the Apostle Peter say in his great Pentecost sermon that "... it was impossible for [Christ] to be held in [death's] power!" I also heard tell of how those same timid disciples who had forsaken him at Calvary were emboldened to stand up to Caiaphas, and despite all his threats, say, "We must obey God rather than any human authority." More than once I was right there in the portico of the Temple cheering them on as they healed and preached fearlessly. That must have been a dismaying sight to the high priest and his cohorts to see Joseph of Arimathea and me, this time on the other side. Perhaps they wanted to put us in the grave like they had wanted to kill Lazarus and return him there? With the spiritual strength of Almighty God surging through our lives, we stood up to be counted for God in another "corrupt generation" not unlike the time in which you are now living.

Listen! The Power and Presence of the Risen Christ which I came to know in the evening of my life you, my friend, can come to know in the morning of your life. I'm telling you, faith in the Risen Christ will both *deliver you and empower you.* Such faith will give you coping power to face and survive all your todays and anything tomorrow may throw at you. Because Christ rose, you see, he walks beside you throughout life! Because Christ rose, he can make you able for anything by strengthening you in the inner person through the Holy Spirit. Because Christ rose, the cross takes away all your sin! Because Christ rose, he awaits you in the Kingdom of Heaven! Because Christ rose, you can *know for sure* that, despite all, "the Lord our God the Almighty *reigns!*" Do you believe this? *Then go out and act upon it!*

Bring Me Up Samuel

A Sermon Preached on Mother's Day

Our Saviour Lutheran Church
Christiansburg, Virginia
May 9, 1999

This sermon with a strange title which, by the way, is a quotation right out of the Bible, is about expressing appreciation. It grows out of one of the saddest stories in the Old Testament. Before we come to that, however, I want to quote for you the memorable ending of what is considered the late Mike Royko's most famous column. This tenderhearted tough-guy concluded this newspaper column in 1979 after his first wife had died of a brain aneurysm with this moving and unforgettable challenge: "If there's someone you love but haven't said so in a while, say it now. Always, always, say it now."

Come back with me now to another time and to a far away place. The time is approximately 1000 B.C., and the place is Israel. There we meet one of the most tragic and pathetic figures in the entire Bible, Saul, the first king of Israel. What makes his story particularly tragic is that he started out so well. When the prophet, Samuel, proclaimed him God's choice for king at Mizpah, he said to the people, "Do you see the one whom the Lord has chosen? *There is no one like him among all the people.*" There was something stately about Saul, for we read in 1 Samuel, "There was not a man among the people of Israel more handsome than he; he stood head and shoulders above everyone else." A modern writer put it, "As he was tall in stature ... there was a tallness in his spirit, a *magnanimity* that would not easily stoop to mean considerations." It is especially important to note that God was with him, for Samuel promised Saul, "The spirit of the Lord will come mightily upon you" (1 Samuel 10:6 RSV). Moreover, Saul was a natural-born leader which he quickly demonstrated as king. Not for nothing,

127

therefore, when he became the first king of Israel, the people shouted enthusiastically, "Long live the king!"

But then, after some years as king, Saul disobeyed God and we read this haunting statement: "The spirit of the Lord departed from Saul" (1 Samuel 16:14). Samuel told him bluntly, "You have rejected the word of the Lord, and the Lord has rejected you from being king over Israel" (1 Samuel 15:23). We don't have time this morning to trace out the disintegration of this soul except to say it started with spiritual disobedience coupled with self-will. What was once a great devotion, shriveled as Saul lost his high commitment to that which was larger than himself. It was a downward spiral from there even into madness as "the spirit of the Lord departed from Saul."

Before it reached this point, however, it is important to remember that Saul had at his beck and call one of the really "good guys" of the Bible. He had Samuel the prophet, but he had stopped listening to him. In the beginning, Samuel had made clear that Saul was chosen by God and called upon to carry out God's will. At the beginning and a long way into his reign, there was a warm stream of affection and helpfulness between Samuel and Saul. The prophet, Samuel, was there at all times to reveal and interpret to the king God's will, but after some time the king thought he knew better than God. As he thus rejected the advice and counsel of Samuel, who was God's spokesman, "The spirit of the Lord departed from Saul."

In the end, when it came to that final battle on Mount Gilboa against the Philistines, Saul was beaten before the battle began. As the battle went against him and after his own sons had fallen, Saul drew his sword and fell upon it, thus ending his life. In words filled with pathos, the Bible states: "Thy glory, O Israel, is slain upon thy high places! *How are the mighty fallen!*" (2 Samuel 1:19).

The night before that disastrous battle, Saul did that which he had decreed no one else should do. Making an exception of himself, he chose to consult a witch. He was that desperate! Saul *desperately* wanted to hear some word from the Lord since by then Samuel was long since gone, and God's Spirit was no longer there

128

to help him. It is an awful thing, my friends, to be thus God-forsaken. In this final pathetic attempt to hear some word of the Lord through the prophet, Saul, under cover of darkness and in disguise, went down to the cave of the witch of Endor. There he begged her to summon up Samuel from the dead, making this pitiful plea, *"Bring me up Samuel."* (1 Samuel 28:11).

Don't let it pass you by that Saul had had Samuel for many years. While he had yet had him, he became unappreciative. Then the king started to disregard the prophet and ultimately he humiliated him. In the early days when Samuel was his guide and counselor and the king had walked uprightly according to God's will, all had gone well with him and with Israel. But when Saul stopped listening to Samuel and threw him over, he began to flounder on alone with growing folly and misfortune as, *"the spirit of the Lord departed from Saul."* He floundered until now, when the final crisis came and Samuel was dead, he pathetically wanted to back up his life and reclaim his lost chances. But it was too late!

"Bring me up Samuel!" as this sad plea reads in the King James Version — *"Bring me up Samuel!"* I sincerely hope this strange sentence will come to haunt you as it has haunted me for years. What this pathetic plea shouts at us is this: *Appreciate your Samuel while such a Godsend is still with you. While you have any Samuel, appreciate him or her and show it before it is too late!* A more practical message could hardly be brought to us on this Mother's Day.

I

This thought, at the very least, ought to stir up within us a fresh appreciation for the significant persons who have been a blessing to our lives. To be sure, through recollection and remembrance, many of these people can be appreciated and learned from even after they have died. We have all been so blessed by significant persons who have warned us against foolishness and have guided us on the right path. But if one of your *Samuels* is still living, run and tell that person of your deep appreciation; tell them what a blessing their life has been to yours; tell them of your love. *"If there's someone you love but haven't said so in a while, say it now. Always, always, say it now."*

This certainly applies to pivotal teachers who have greatly influenced our lives. Have you ever gone out of your way to thank such a teacher? I had a splendid opportunity to do just that several years ago when our seminary class gathered at Wittenberg University in Springfield, Ohio, for our fortieth reunion. I was chosen by my classmates to be the Master of Ceremonies at a luncheon. As such, Mary and I were privileged to sit alone at a table with our honored speaker, Dr. T. A. Kantonen, and his wife Frances. Dr. Kantonen, a giant of a man in the Lutheran Church, was the best professor any seminary student could ever have. He was then 93 years old and still sharp as a tack. Across the table that day I told this master teacher and great Christian how much he had influenced my life. I told him what a blessing he had been to my ministry. His three years of lectures introduced me as nothing else to the grace-theology of the Bible. After I was in a parish, he was never too busy to write me personal letters with helpful answers to my questions. Even that day as we sat together in a private dining room, I sought his answer to a question on Christian ethics which had long perplexed me. Then, too, his books have greatly influenced my ministry. One titled *The Resurgence of the Gospel*, more than I could tell you this morning, has been incorporated into my whole approach to ministry. And to say these things is not even to begin to speak of the Christian example this man set as his life brushed across mine. That day over lunch I had a splendid chance to thank him for being my teacher. Moreover, that day I also had the privilege of standing up before my greying colleagues in the clergy and introducing this master teacher they knew so well and then publicly honoring and thanking one of the best *Samuels* any of us have ever had. Whereupon the class rose to give this old man a warm and lengthy standing applause. In God's timing, he died shortly thereafter, but not before knowing what a profound effect his life had on the class of '52.

It is also appropriate, I believe, to express appreciation to faithful pastors. We have all had significant pastors during the living of our days who, through their words and example, have ministered to us and helped change our lives. The day after Dick Sheppard died, a distinguished British minister, a London morning paper was inspired to express this truth unforgettably. The newspaper carried a photograph of the pulpit at St. Martin's where this prophet had spoken so many times and described that pulpit in these words: "The steps wound beautifully round, as ever, and a beam of light shown softly down on the reading desk." On this pulpit the Bible was lying open. In the margin of the picture the editor printed by hand these words: "Here endeth the first lesson." If your life has been blessed with such a minister, make haste to tell that person while you yet can how God has worked through him or her to bless your life.

Most of all, expressing love and appreciation is applicable to beloved parents. If we should find ways to express our appreciation to teachers and pastors, how much more is this true in regard to our own parents. Granted that neither we nor they are perfect, how many opportunities do we, nevertheless, overlook just to say thanks to mothers and fathers who brought us into the world and cared for us and nurtured us and sacrificed for us and, when we were ready, let go and released us out into the world? One woman, who nearly lost her elderly mother, didn't miss this chance to write a moving letter of gratitude. I want to quote a few abbreviated excerpts from that splendid letter with the hope that it will cause you this day to go home and do the same for your living parents.

Dear Mama,

It is Sunday night and I just can't sleep. I keep thanking God that we did not lose you last month and that you seem to be making a good recovery. I hope this continues.

Many times in the past weeks I have wondered if you know how much I love and admire you. I know I have not been good at telling you that with words and it just hit me in the hospital how much you mean to all of us.

Much of the time the first few days I just sat quietly beside your bed and kept my hand on your head ... I knew you had come through the surgery well, but I thought of how fragile life is for all of us and that I better say now what is in my heart. [This woman then

went on to list thirteen different things for which she
was thankful. Among them are the following]:

*... I want to thank you for leading me to a strong faith
in God ...*
*... I want to thank you for modeling the strength of this
belief during very rough times ...*
*Thank you for teaching me the wonder and beauty of a
family ...*
*Thank you for giving me a thirst for knowledge. I don't
think it will ever be quenched ...*
*Thank you for teaching me to be a woman and to be
happy being one ...*
*Thank you for making the great hymns of the church
our natural music. How often it bears me up on eagles'
wings ...*

[The letter continues and then ends in this way]: *I hope
we have many years left together, but I wanted you to
know some of what you have meant to me and how
dearly you are loved.*

It was my dear wife, Mary, who wrote this letter two years ago.
She also read it in its entirety in the church at her mother's funeral
only two months ago. *"If there's someone you love but haven't
said so in a while, say it now. Always, always, say it now."*

There are, of course, other *Samuels* we might mention: spouses,
relatives, friends, co-workers, church members. Let us not miss
the opportunities we have to say thanks to them while they are still
alive. Let us not follow in the footsteps of Saul who after it was too
late went down to the cave of the witch of Endor and pled pathetically, *"Bring me up Samuel!"* God save us all from that!

II

**At the very least, as I have been saying, this penetrating
sentence ought to stir up profound appreciation for the significant persons who have influenced our lives.** How much more
ought this be true of our appreciation for Jesus Christ, the Lord of
the Church. At the Baptism of Jesus, a voice from Heaven said,

132

"This is my Son, the Beloved, with whom I am well pleased." My friends, the greatest *Samuel* any of us could ever have is God's Anointed, the Lord Jesus Christ. If you love him, why not somehow say so? *"If there's someone you love but haven't said so in a while, say it now. Always, always, say it now."*

One of the things I particularly like about this church building is the nave. Our worship space is so bright and cheerful especially because of the clerestory windows. Moreover, our clear side windows blend the outside with the inside suggesting that God is present in both. Sometimes I use my church key to come here in private in order to pray and also to ponder the symbolism as I always do on Sunday mornings as well. Have you ever noticed how this church speaks eloquently of Christ when no one is speaking?

Note, for example, the Star of Bethlehem above the manger depicted in the window to your left. You will recall that, after consulting with bad King Herod, the Wise Men, as the record reads, "set out; and there, ahead of them, went the star ... until it stopped over the place where the child was." And what did they do when they got there? "They fell down and worshiped him" (Matthew 2:9, 11 RSV). I thus hear an important message in the symbolism of the church when no one is speaking. Then note further the processional cross positioned behind the altar for our eyes to catch. I love to watch that cross when it is carried into our nave at the beginning of worship and placed there. It draws our eyes and casts its shadow, as it were, upon the manger scene and the star in the window. That is why Christ came, to die on Calvary's Cross for us and our salvation. From the beginning, God had a plan for us, and it centered in a Cross. Saint Paul tells us about that as he wrote, "God shows his love for us in that while we were yet sinners Christ died for us" (Romans 5:8 RSV). The symbolism which is before us thus breaks again into silent speech. Then let your eyes fall upon the window to your right where the red and white banner with a cross rises out of the empty tomb. This is the banner of victory which reminds us of the Lord's glorious victory at Easter. Through this symbolism Christ himself is speaking even now to us this triumphant and reassuring word: "I am the resurrection and the life. Those who believe in me, even though they die, will live, and everyone who lives and believes in me will never die" (John 11:25). Still another silent sermon is being preached to us in this sanctuary. Then in this same window beneath the dove of the Spirit, notice the sevenfold tongues of fire. This causes me to think of the apostles on the Day of Pentecost, the birthday of the Church, when Peter, filled with the Holy Spirit, preached a compelling sermon which could not be held in, underscoring, in effect, the biblical Truth that, "... no one can say 'Jesus is Lord' except by the Holy Spirit." And thus through the beauty of symbolism still another powerful though unspoken message reaches my soul. Altogether, these symbols and others here in this sanctuary undergird some words in our First Reading today wherein it stands written that God "is not far from each one of us...." Indeed! As we sang earlier, "God is here! As we, God's people, meet to offer praise and prayer."

All this and more come together in the workmanship of the Holy Spirit which is the Church of Jesus Christ. Here in the Church of Christ as "Children of the Heavenly Father," we are received into membership through Holy Baptism. Here in the Church of Christ in study and in worship the Spirit brings us to faith as we come to deeply understand words that children sing: "Jesus loves me, this I know; for the Bible tells me so." Here in the Church of Christ we receive assurance of the forgiveness of sins as we partake of the Lord's Supper. Here in the Church of Christ, among many other happenings, we take our marriage vows in God's presence, fellowship with believers in our common Savior, grow in the our faith and life through the inspiration of the Holy Spirit, and bid a final farewell to those who have been called forth into the Kingdom of Heaven. So should we not, therefore, say with zest and enthusiasm that which the Psalmist said, "I was glad when they said to me, 'Let us go into the house of the Lord!' " (Psalm 122:1).

And Christ himself is the *supreme Samuel*, the ever-present Lord of the Church, who, above all, should not only be appreciated but thanked with our lives. Thanking him with our lives — that's how we can appropriately express our love for him. The Lord Jesus Christ, who is in our midst right now, "is not far from each one of us." Do we love him as we ought to love? Are we willing to give him back the life we owe? Do we even fully recognize his living presence among us?

Some of us here now may still be out there on that Emmaus Road where those two disciples were on the first Easter evening when, according to the Scripture, "Jesus himself came near and went with them, but their eyes were kept from recognizing him" (Luke 24:15). Well, when I read that story, I want to shake those two disciples and say, "What's the matter with you two? Don't you realize that Christ has indeed risen from the dead and is talking to you right now?" But some here may well be still back on that Emmaus Road. My friends, the Living Christ is even more with us now than Samuel was with Saul for many years, but all too often like Saul we neither take God's Word as seriously as we ought nor appreciate His presence as we should. Otherwise, we would not get so tangled up in the business of life that we sometimes ignore Him. Otherwise we would not become so consumed with ourselves that sometimes we stifle the still small voice of God. But through it all, Jesus Christ, the Lord of the Church, the greatest Samuel of all, is here now speaking to us, reaching out to us, loving us, trying to save us, guiding us, and strengthening us in our inner being through the Spirit. Thank God, that story of the disciples on the Emmaus Road comes to the point, as Saint Luke records it, that, "Their eyes were opened, and they recognized him." Hear that well: *"Their eyes were opened, and they recognized him."*

Would that that would happen to someone here today. Would that someone here today would go home from this service knowing as never before that Christ himself is present in our midst and ever-ready to bless us. Should we not therefore appropriately thank him with our love? After all, "If there's someone you love — especially Christ! — if there's someone you love, but haven't said so in a while, say it now. Always, always, say it now." An old familiar hymn asks, "Sinner, do you love my Jesus?" And the answer comes, "If you love him, why not serve him?" Why, then, not love him and serve him "with all your heart, and with all your soul, and with all your mind"? And why might we do this? Let the Apostle John answer: "We love because he first loved us."

135

Well, Saul had had his Samuel though he wasted many chances to demonstrate his appreciation. But we here still have many *Samuels* and especially the greatest *Samuel* of all, the Lord Jesus Christ. *God keep us*, every one, from throwing our chances away. *God help us,* every one, to heed God's Word and to listen to His invitations as well as to His warnings. *God save us*, every one, from waiting too long and then one day having to go down to some Endor's cave and somehow cry out as pitifully as did Saul, *"Bring me up Samuel!"* God save us all from that!

If I Had Only One Sermon To Preach!

A Sermon Preached on the Occasion of an Adult Baptism

Our Saviour Lutheran Church
Christiansburg, Virginia
September 12, 1999

It has been a joy and a privilege for me as a pastor to cradle in my arms more than a thousand small children to baptize them "in the Name of the Father, and of the Son, and of the Holy Spirit." It has also been a joy to baptize adults, who, somehow having missed receiving the Sacrament as a child, have come in their maturity to the baptismal font to profess their own personal faith in Jesus Christ as Savior and Lord. Consequently, this is not only a special day for Jimmy and his family. It is also a special day for me as a retired pastor not serving a congregation as I may never again have the high privilege of officiating at either an infant or an adult Baptism. Therefore, thank you, Jimmy, for asking me to share with you in this service, and I say to you again from the heart for myself and for all of us here, "We welcome you into the Lord's family. We receive you as [a fellow member] of the body of Christ, [a child] of the same heavenly Father, and [a worker] with us in the Kingdom of God."

Now the Bible teaches that Baptism is important, urgent, and even essential. Jesus said, "The one who believes and is baptized, will be saved!" That is a precious promise, but remember the Master went right on to say, "... the one who does not believe will be condemned" (Mark 16:16). As Saint Paul reminds us in today's Second Lesson, one day "... we will all stand before the judgment seat of God ... each of us will be accountable to God." This suggests that a static and sterile belief will not suffice. What we do need is a growing faith in order to be ever-ready to enter into the kingdom of Heaven.

I ask you, is *anything* more important than that? Does *anything* matter more than our eternal destiny? Does wealth which we cannot take with us? Does popularity which is so fickle? Does success which comes and goes like the tides of the sea? Does even a healthy body which can be ours today but gone tomorrow? Nothing compares with the importance of our eternal salvation! "The one who **believes** (that is, who trusts in the saving grace of Christ the Lord and then thanks God with his or her life) — *The one who believes and is Baptized **will** be saved!*" To be thus among the saved matters above all else!

To underscore further the importance of this matter, suppose today that I have only this one last sermon to preach to a worshiping congregation. Suppose I will never again get another chance to stand in a pulpit and proclaim the gospel. Suppose that after the service today I should have to take off my clergy robes forever. What might I say in such a situation? There will come a day not too many years into the future when I am no longer able to preach. Before that time sweeps in upon me, however, I want to be absolutely sure that I have said quite clearly what this world so desperately needs to hear said.

But at any time in one's life, it is a sobering discipline for a Christian preacher to imagine he or she has only one sermon to preach! What might that ordained servant say? What is the *essential message* of Scripture? What is the *irreducible minimum* of Christianity? What — to use Jeremiah's words — is that *"fire shut up in (his) bones"*? (20:9). Such an imaginary discipline, you see, forces a preacher back to the core of the Christian faith. And more: it gives that preacher a sense of urgency not unlike that of Richard Baxter who said, "I preached as never sure to preach again, and as a dying man to dying men." At my ordination in Joliet, Illinois in 1952, the President of the Synod read these words from Romans: "For whosoever shall call upon the name of the Lord shall be saved. How then shall they call on him in whom they have not believed? And how shall they call on him in whom they have not heard? And how shall they hear without a preacher?" (10:13-14 KJV). Imagine with me that this is my *last* chance to proclaim the gospel and you people just *happen* to be here today.

But then suppose further that this is to be the last sermon that *you* will ever hear. Who knows when the call up yonder might come?

How, therefore, will you listen? Will you just fiddle with your bulletin, or daydream, or will you *really* listen? Then how will you respond? What difference might such a sermon make in your life? If, let us say, the *preacher* manages to get the message right, will *you* then receive it rightly?

Were this the last sermon I could ever preach, I would most certainly stress that the word "gospel" means "good news." Consequently, I wish now to underline and accentuate three pieces of this really good news and to do so *quite emphatically*.

I

First, if I had only one sermon to preach, **I would most definitely proclaim the tremendous good news of Salvation**. I would not trouble you with systematic theology or church practice. No! Straightaway I would put the trumpet to my lips, as it were, and blare forth that Jesus Christ is the Savior. I would remind you that even if you have failed God *miserably,* even if you have missed the mark *widely,* even if you have been untrue to yourself *terribly,* and even if you have let down your friends and family *sadly,* nevertheless — *nevertheless,* God still loves you, is ever anxious to forgive you, and is always willing to give you a fresh start. This is His promise to us, His covenant or contract with us, in the Sacrament of Holy Baptism. Baptism affirms God's unbreakable promise to us humans to be willing always to love and forgive us into becoming better Christians. In eloquent words from a sermon by my late brother-in-law, the Reverend Dr. J. Schoneberg Setzer, it is as though God said, "I am now promising to hear you [through] your whole life when you cry to me for forgiveness. No matter how grave or deep the evil you fall into, no matter how far you stray from my Dear Son's Church, I promise you when you ask for forgiveness in his Name, it will always be yours. My Son's Blessed Sacrifice upon the Cross has already blotted out every evil you will ever be or do." If I just had one chance to speak with you, I would want you to know that you are never beyond the reach of God's love.

Sin, after all, is the biggest problem any of us face. As David said, "... my sin is ever before me." We walk through this world on the clay feet of our humanity, saying with Saint Paul, "I do not do the good I want, but the evil I do not want is what I do" (Romans 7:15 RSV). What honest person here has never felt that? Moreover, each of us has some special weakness, that which Hebrews calls, "the sin which doth so easily beset us" (12:1 KJV). It might be temper, greed, pride, lust, selfishness, lying, drugs — you name it. The old devil certainly knows how to get through to each of us *individually*. A person would have to be self-deceived not to acknowledge that or to be able to say with King David, "I know my transgressions, and *my sin is ever before me*" (Psalm 51:3).

But the New Testament, in fulfillment of the Old Testament, is written around the central theme of saviorhood. The towering figure of the Gospels is the promised Messiah who came, so it stands written, "to save his people from their sins." Jesus explained His earthly mission quite clearly, saying, "God so loved the world, that he gave his only begotten Son, that whosoever believeth in him should not perish, but have everlasting life" (John 3:16 KJV). Throughout his ministry the Master said repeatedly in one way or another to all who would listen, "Your sins are forgiven. Go and sin no more" (John 8:11). The result was freedom from the condemnation of sin as stated by the Apostle Paul: "There is therefore now no condemnation for those who are in Christ Jesus" (Romans 8:1). All this is ours through faith in Christ, for the pathway to salvation is just as simple as Paul and Silas said it was to the Philippian jailer, "Believe in the Lord Jesus Christ, and you will be saved" (Acts 16:31). But note that immediately thereafter, so Acts 16 tells us, that jailer "... and his entire family were baptized without delay" (16:33). *"Without delay!"* Do you catch the sense of urgency here?

Some years ago a 24-year-old electrical engineer was called home to aid his pregnant wife who had been injured in her kitchen. In a terrible hurry he alighted from his commuter train at Berwyn, Illinois, and, crossing the tracks, went quickly around the last car right into the pathway of the speeding Denver Zephyr heading into Chicago. I was a passenger on the train that killed him! Who knows what a day will bring? But this we do know, as the Bible plainly states it, *"Now is the acceptable time; see now is the day of salvation!"* (2 Corinthians 6:2).

II

Second, if I had only one sermon to preach, **I would most certainly herald the unprecedented good news of the Resurrection**.This historic reality changed everything. Even the Cross was thereby completely transformed from a symbol of infamy into a symbol of glory! Moreover, without the resurrection, there would have been no Church, no New Testament, no salvation, no Heaven. That first Easter made everything different. When that angel said to the disciples, "He has risen, he is not here," (Luke 24:5 RSV) the dawn of hope came into this darkened world. If I had just one opportunity to seize your attention, I would certainly tell you the good news that Jesus Christ is risen from the dead and lives and reigns in all eternity.

Don't let it pass you by that the Resurrection is a mighty reinforcing fact of life. The unshakable fact of the Resurrection has nerved the followers of Christ all through the centuries. Because Christ rose, there is comfort enough to *dry our tears.* Because Christ rose, there is victory enough to *make us more than conquerors.* Because Christ rose, there is hope enough to *see us through anything.* Because Christ rose, there is certainty enough to *fling wide the gates of eternity.* Christianity is *the* religion of resurrection. We can therefore rejoice. Here, if anywhere, is good news worth shouting about!

But, you must see, too, that the Resurrection also makes a profound difference in the way we die. Only this last week I telephoned and talked with a former parishioner and old personal friend of over forty years. This good man is now near death of bone cancer in Memorial Hospital in Carthage, Illinois. Both Mary and I as well as our friend, Mylon, became emotional as we realized we may never speak again in this world. We talked, therefore, about our common faith in God as well as the hope we share in Christ for life after death. I then went out of my way to thank him for his salutary influence on my life. Then he said this: "I am not afraid to die. I can look death in the eye because I have already done so." Well he had! First, his beautiful and athletically-gifted son tragically drowned in the Kootenai River one summer while he was working in Montana. Then his dear wife Virginia, the best friend

141

my wife ever had, died of cancer in her forties. When he finally remarried trying to start again, his second wife was killed in an automobile accident. And then just last November when we saw Mylon out in Illinois where I spoke, he had only recently stood by the grave of one of his dear daughters who had died of the same cancer which had taken her mother. More than most of us, he has looked death in the eye. Now after battling cancer himself for four years, he himself is nearing the end and he knows it. Still he said to us with courage and unflinching faith, "I am not afraid to die." Where do we get men like that? In the Church of Christ, that's where, for in that fellowship of believers this man came to know Jesus as Savior, Lord, and Friend above all others. Don't miss in the hymn we have just sung, the meaningful words the hymn-writer, John Ylvisaker, put into the mouth of God. Listen ...

> *I was there to hear your borning cry,*
> *I'll be there when you are old.*
> *I rejoiced the day you were baptized,*
> *to see your life unfold ...*

> [And then further] *When evening gently closes in*
> *and you shut your weary eyes,*
> *I'll be there as I have always been*
> *with just one more surprise.*[1]

On Easter Sunday in 1955, I was too sick with a debilitating kidney infection to stand in my pulpit in Lena, Illinois, but not sick enough to stay home from church. Therefore, being dreadfully weak, I went to church with my wife Mary but had to remain seated throughout the service and leave early, as I wasn't strong enough to shake hands with anybody. The service was conducted by the beloved Reverend Dr. Harmon J. McGuire, who had ordained me three years previously. This dear man, affectionately known as "Pat," was then President of the Illinois Synod of the old United Lutheran Church. To tell the truth, I don't remember anything Dr. McGuire said in his sermon — a humbling thought for a preacher! — but I shall never forget his concluding words. He spoke of the joys of Heaven and told the congregation how he looked forward to going there one day and seeing his Lord face to face and being reunited with his loved ones who had gone ahead. Then with a suddenness and loudness that was startling — in fact, *astounding!* — he threw his hands into the air, gazed upward, and ended the sermon abruptly with a single loud word: "HALLELUJAH!" My friends, that was the last Easter sermon "Pat" McGuire ever preached. He died shortly thereafter, but this dear man was ready. Are you? If you are not, I wouldn't let the sun go down today without surrendering your life to Jesus Christ as risen Lord and Savior.

III

Finally, if I had only one sermon to preach, **I would most assuredly accent the reinforcing good news of faith's Empowerment**. In short, people, the effect of the Christian faith is real! True, Christ came into this world bringing salvation. True, he rose from the dead to open up the gateway to Heaven. But when we press this matter yet further, Christ also gave us the Holy Spirit to empower us to live wisely and well in the here and now. Thus, Christ enters into us as a partner in living the Christian life. Not for nothing, therefore, are we baptized in the Name of the Triune God, that is, "in the Name of the Father, and of the Son, *and of the Holy Spirit.*" Don't let this be lost on you! Through the Spirit, you see, Christ is alive and active in our daily lives. It is the Spirit, for instance, who enables us to discern between right and wrong and then to go God's way. It is the Spirit who gives us the internal fortitude necessary to stand up to life. What is more, Christ's Spirit gives us an undiscourageable good will, a wholesome attitude, and an unconquerable optimism as we live out our faith. If I had but one crack at you, I would certainly want you to know how readily available is the immense power of the Holy Spirit to strengthen you and to change your life.

Who among us here at times during life has not been simply overwhelmed? Who here has not from time to time been severely tempted to take the low road? Who here has not sometimes been all stressed-out? Who here has not at least occasionally felt totally inadequate to cope with life. There are plenty of things in this world that can get us down and do us in. But the point is we are never alone. Christ is alive and with us. This is the inevitable result, you see, of his rising from the dead. Through the Holy Spirit, Christ himself is standing beside you to keep you from falling. He is there to help you see clearly the consequences of bad choices. And he is ever ready to walk with you into whatever future lies ahead. I do not think the enormous practicality of the Christian faith has been emphasized nearly enough. On his knees Paul prayed that all Christians might "be strengthened in [the] inner being with power through [the] Spirit" (Ephesians 3:16). There is, therefore, now a power in Christ's Spirit that *gives* us the courage to just say, "No," that *makes* us resilient enough to bounce back from failure, that *empowers* us to keep on keeping on even when we feel like quitting, that *enables* us to look into the jaws of adversity and keep smiling, and above all, that *helps* us to see life through to the finish victoriously. The Holy Spirit, who strengthens us in our inner being, does all that and more. No stranger to tough times, Saint Paul could therefore in chains from a prison cell pen these magnificent words: "In him who strengthens me I am able for *anything*!" (Philippians 4:13 James Moffatt translation).

Only last month there was a memorable episode in my favorite comic strip about that valiant but very human Viking, *Hagar the Horrible*. Hagar's old daddy called his son to the top of the hill of wisdom to share with him one great secret of life, a secret, so he said, which had taken him 75 years to learn. The old man says to Hagar, "Lean closer, son, and I'll whisper the secret to you." "Great!" says Hagar. And then he asks eagerly, "What is it, Dad! What is it?" Whereupon the old man reveals this great secret, which is this: "Life is tough!" Well, Hagar's face showed he already knew that! And so do we! This being true, what we need is God's abiding presence *with us* coupled with God's all-mighty power *in us*. My friends, this is what the Holy Spirit does!

Let me once more move with this into the first person singular, as somehow I must in order to bear my testimony. In my life, to begin with, I have sometimes been assailed by doubts about the Christian faith as well as about myself, but the Spirit of Christ has enabled me to go all the way through with my doubts until I came out on the other side with a stronger faith hearing anew the words of Jesus, "I am with you always." In my life, as an example, I have experienced grief so deep that it has rocked me back on my heels, but the Spirit of Christ has made it possible for me to smile through my tears as I heard his uplifting words, "Be of good cheer, I have overcome the world" (John 16:33 RSV). In my life, as another example, I have been so bombarded by pressure and at times been so close to burnout that I wondered not "if" but "when" I would no longer be able to take it and would thus cave in and crack up, but then the Spirit of Christ caused me to hear again the Master's words, "My power is made perfect in weakness" (2 Corinthians 12:9 RSV). In my life, furthermore, I have been called upon to undertake responsibilities so great that I thought I was way over my head and I trembled at the thought of being found out, but the Spirit of Christ said to me as he said to Joshua, "Be strong and of good courage; be not frightened, neither be dismayed; for the Lord your God is with you wherever you go" (Joshua 1:9 RSV). In my life, again, I have been knocked down so hard that I thought I would never be able to get up, but then the Spirit of Christ entered into me so that I could say with Ezekiel, "The Spirit entered into me and set me upon my feet" (3:24). In my life, still again, I have occasionally been so inundated by discouragement that I have even considered quitting the ministry, but the Eternal God through the Spirit of Christ came alongside of me as I read God's word to Jeremiah which burned away the fog of his discouragement and put starch into his soul, "Before I formed you in the womb I knew you [and] I appointed you a prophet" (1:5). Hear then again those invigorating words of the apostle: "In [Christ] who strengthens me I am able for anything!" Isn't it about time you, too, tap into a power like that? Only so will you be able, in Isaiah's words, to "run and not be weary," but short of that, as least, as so often has been the case with me, just to be able to "walk and not faint" (Isaiah 40:31). Do not, I beg you, impede the inrush of God's Spirit.

So there you have it as best I can put if I had only one sermon to preach as I have spoken with you about *salvation*, *resurrection*, and *empowerment*. Now, it is up to you. Now *you* must either accept Christ or reject him; *you* must either bow down your life before him in uttermost surrender or turn away. But, friend, consider this: it is *your* eternal destiny which is at stake here. As today's Epistle reminds us, "We will all stand before the judgment seat of God ... each of us will be accountable to God" (Romans 14:10, 12). Moreover, not only must we all be baptized, as Christ commanded; we must also believe strongly enough to follow through with a kind of faith that changes our lives. So I ask you today, *do you get the message?*

---

1. Used by permission. ©1985 John Ylvisaker, Box 321, Waverly, Iowa 50677.

Why I Am A Lutheran

A Sermon for Reformation Sunday

Our Saviour Lutheran Church
Christiansburg, Virginia
October 31, 1999

Lest we lose our perspective, I want to begin with an anecdote. There is a town in Norway named H-E-L-L, Hell. Because of its unusual name this town draws many tourists. A while back a Lutheran couple from Georgia visited there and sent a postcard home to their pastor. This cleric drew much laughter when he read that card to the local ministerial association. "Dear pastor," it said, "we passed through Hell today, and we're concerned. Almost everyone here seems to be Lutheran."

It is with no desire to be exclusive or elitist that I have chosen to speak on this Reformation Sunday on the subject, "Why I am a Lutheran." An aloof or superior attitude is totally inappropriate and even un-Christian in the modern ecumenical climate when Christians of all persuasions are reaching out in love to touch one another and to discover their oneness in Christ. In fact, on this very day Lutherans and Catholics are signing in Augsburg, Germany, a "Joint Declaration on the Doctrine of Justification" thereby agreeing on a common statement of justification and a mutual lifting of the condemnations of one another that have existed for four hundred and seventy years. My friends, there is so much common ground in Christianity and so much we can learn from other churches.

Personally speaking, I could easily proliferate examples. One of the finest theological volumes in my library, for instance, is titled *A Faith to Proclaim* by the late Dr. James S. Stewart, a distinguished Scotch Presbyterian. Moreover, the absolute best sermon I have ever heard on justification by faith was given in North Carolina in 1955 by Colin Williams, a then-famous Australian Methodist. Furthermore, one of the most inspiring hours of my lifetime was spent privately in my Philadelphia church study after a wedding with a spiritual giant who had assisted me, a clergyman who was a confidant of popes and presidents, a familiar television figure of the day and longtime President of the University of Notre Dame, the Rev. Father Theodore M. Hesburgh, a great Roman Catholic. What I am saying here is that, far from deprecating other churches of Christendom, I salute them with gratitude for their contributions to our understanding of the Christian Faith. I encourage you to do likewise.

For all that, I feel I have a right and a responsibility to *think through* and to *profess why* I choose to be a Lutheran. It seems to me that any serious Christian would want to do the same whatever his or her denomination. My reasons for being a Lutheran may differ from yours, but I suspect they will be complementary, not contradictory.

For reasons of time, however, I cannot say everything this morning I would like to say. Even what I will be saying must be briefly put. Were it a live option today, I would speak at some length about my deep appreciation for our liturgy which so meaningfully blends Word and Sacrament. I could put in a good word for our strong educational program which grows out of Bible study and the catechism. I could also attest to the biblical authenticity of our Spirit-inspired Lutheran style of evangelism. I could speak today further of our understanding as Lutheran Christians of the meaning of stewardship which, simply put, is this: "I give thee back the life I owe," and, "God shovels in and we shovel out, but God has the bigger shovel." I could state much appreciation for the prominence and importance of the laity in the life and worship of our Lutheran Church. I could also recount how the Lutheran Church has been in the vanguard of the ecumenical movement among Protestants and Catholics alike. I could, moreover, make a whole sermon about the freedom from sin and death that is ours in Christ as our Lord states in today's Gospel, "You will know the truth, and the truth will make you free," and then further, "If the Son makes you free, you will be free indeed." These are just some of the directions we could go with today's subject.

148

But rather than pursuing any of these aforementioned strengths of our Church, I want today to emphasize one central point and then to illustrate it in five ways. Why am I a Lutheran? *The pre-eminent reason why I am a Lutheran is Lutheran theology!* It is not enough for me or anyone to say, "I am a Lutheran because I was born one," though that is not an unfortunate event. It is not enough to have had an overpowering Christian experience, though that is a real blessing. We Lutherans are thinking people, you see, which means there must be no cerebral by-pass. Speaking for myself, therefore, *it was the biblical, Christ-centered theology which long ago hooked me* and about which I wish to speak this morning.

First, as Lutherans, ours is a theology which recognizes and appreciates *God's initiative*! Our theology recognizes and appreciates God's initiative. A few years ago, a popular bumper sticker said, "I found it!" I know and understand what these good people were trying to say, but still I must point out that the statement, "I found it!" is theologically indefensible. For one thing, "it" is impersonal, whereas our faith is placed in a personal God. For another thing, that slogan puts the emphasis and initiative, wrongly, on us as human beings. " '*I*' found it!" Ever and always in the history of salvation, it must be said that "*He* found us!" God always took the initiative, made humankind His children, ran after them when they strayed, and wooed them into the fold. God showed up unexpectedly, for example, in Haran and called Abraham to be the father of His people. He appeared to the Children of Israel in the person of Moses out in Egypt when they were forlorn and discouraged and brought deliverance. He kept sending prophets when the Israelites were wicked and rebellious and forgetful to tell them He loved them still. And at last, He surprised the world with the kind of Messiah this sin-sick world really needs. So the Almighty God reaches out and runs after us still, always, *always* taking the initiative.

Here is the key to our Lutheran understanding of the sacrament of infant Baptism. It is *all* God's doing! Before we are old enough, wise enough, strong enough, or good enough to come to God, *He lovingly comes to us and makes us His children.* In infant Baptism, God's gift of grace precedes our effort, our study, even

149

our understanding. He takes the initial step, seeking us before we seek Him. God comes to the helpless infant and gives Himself. The Lord God Almighty brings that tiny child into the Kingdom of God and promises eternal life through Jesus Christ. He who is the sovereign ruler of the endless stretches of the universe comes in love to one small person at the baptismal font. Thus, infant Baptism is a unique summary of the whole doctrine of justification by grace through faith.

That kind of divine initiative runs all the way through Lutheran theology. Nowhere is that more clearly put than by Luther in his explanation to the Third Article of the Creed: "I believe," wrote the Reformer in *The Small Catechism,* "I believe that I cannot by my own understanding or effort believe in Jesus Christ my Lord, or come to Him. But the Holy Spirit has called me through the gospel." Mark it: *Not by our own understanding or effort do we come to Christ, but the Holy Spirit reaches out to us and calls us through the gospel!* Thus, God Himself is reaching out to us throughout our lives to make us His very own. He keeps coming to us through the gospel. He enters into us as we are given his body and blood for the forgiveness of sins at the Lord's Table. And the Spirit of Christ seeks us out whenever we stray. There is just no way we can ever get beyond that "love that will not let [us] go." All this, you see, underscores God's initiative. I'm not saying that other churches don't say this as well, but for me, the Lutheran Church says it best. Ours is a theology which recognizes and appreciates God's initiative.

Second, as Lutherans ours is a theology which is rooted and grounded in *God's word*! Our theology is rooted and grounded in God's Word. Our Lord himself in the temptation experience countered each of the three onslaughts of the devil by saying, "It is written" and then quoted the Scripture. On the Cross Jesus quoted the Psalm 22. He knew it by heart. From the beginning to the end of his ministry our Lord was constantly quoting what we know as the Old Testament. Furthermore, he said, "Heaven and earth will pass away, but my words will not pass away" (Matthew 24:35). So the apostles in the first century to Christians in the twentieth century have tucked away in their memory boxes precious verses of the Bible. It is no wonder, therefore, that The Formula of Concord, one of our Lutheran Confessions, begins with these words: "We believe, teach, and confess that the only rule and guiding principle according to which all teachings and teachers are to be evaluated and judged are the prophetic and apostolic writings of the Old and New Testament alone."

This is not to say that we Lutherans read the Bible with rigid literalism. We are *not* fundamentalists. In many instances, you must realize, the Bible does *not* take *itself* literally. In the ninth chapter of Judges, for example, Jotham gives a speech atop Mount Gerizim. It is biting satire at its best, and the point is well made that there is danger of losing the kingship of God by seeking out an earthly king. It would therefore be ridiculous to take literally what Jotham said about olive trees and brambles. To do so would be to miss the point entirely. Over in the New Testament Jesus said, "It is easier for a camel to go through the eye of a needle than for someone who is rich to enter the kingdom of God" (Matthew 19:24). That is clearly speaking in hyperbole, but the point is well made that riches can be perilous to one's salvation. To get hung up on trying to perceive how a camel could possibly go through the eye of a needle would be ridiculous. When we cannot take the Bible literally, however, we can most certainly take it *seriously.* The Good Book is profoundly relevant to our faith and our way of life. As we read in Hebrews, according to the Phillips translation, "For the Word that God speaks is alive and active: it cuts more keenly than any two edged sword: it strikes through to the place where soul and spirit meet, to the innermost intimacies of [one's] being: it exposes the very thoughts and motives of a [person's] heart. No creature has any cover from the sight of God...." Mark this, therefore: one can take the Bible very seriously indeed without taking everything in the Good Book literally.

As we approach the Word of God from this *reverent* and *relevant* point of view, it moves right off the pages and out into life. The Bible becomes, if I may put it so, "bigger than big." Men and women may sadly argue back and forth, for example, about whether the world was created in six 24-hour days. To do so, however, runs the risk of missing the whole point of Genesis 1 — namely, God

Almighty *is* the creator, however long He may have taken to do that. As it stands written: "In the beginning God created the heavens and the earth" (Genesis 1:1). The profound consequences of that for our faith in the eternal God and for our stewardship of life will never run out! Again, in that happy hunting ground for heretics, the Book of Revelation, people sometimes find all kinds of wild and crazy things. To do this sort of baseless conjecturing, however, runs the risk of missing the whole point of the last book of the Bible — namely, God is more powerful than Rome or anything else. Listen to the sixth verse of the nineteenth chapter: "Hallelujah! For the Lord our God the Almighty reigns." The profound encouragement in those words is like a deep well that will never run dry! All of what we are saying here underscores the power and potency of God's Word. I'm not saying at all that other churches don't take the Bible seriously, but for me the Lutheran Church is more consistent and more balanced in this emphasis. Ours is a theology which is rooted and grounded in God's Word.

Third, as Lutherans ours is a theology which makes central and focal *God's salvation*! Our theology makes central and focal God's salvation. From the beginning, God's eternal plan of salvation was destined to culminate on Calvary's Cross whereupon the only begotten Son of God gave his life's blood for humankind. We need only believe he died there for us in order to be saved. Though we are all sinners, as our Second Lesson for this Reformation Sunday makes plain, nevertheless, we are — I'm quoting our lesson now — "justified by his grace as a gift, through the redemption that is in Christ Jesus, whom God put forward as a sacrifice of atonement by his blood, effective through faith" (Romans 3:24-25). Justified by grace through faith in Jesus Christ — that was the rallying theme of the Reformation. The hymnist, Toplady, put it as plainly and simply as it can be put: "Thou must save, and thou alone."

This differs from all earthbound religion. Most people's conception of Christianity is legalistic and moralistic. The most common religion of our time, both inside and outside the Church, is the false religion of good works. People fully expect to be saved on their record. But such is impossible! We simply cannot ever be good enough for God's Heaven or even to help out with our salvation. Back in the mid-'50s, we bought for our children a horizontal ladder or what you possibly might call "monkey bars." It was twelve feet across, and we installed it in the ground in such a way that, even with my height, I could easily swing across hand over hand. One day one of my daughters, seeing a long pole lying in the yard, asked me if I could touch the sky with that pole from the top of that horizontal ladder. Well, I went along with it. I climbed to the top, which must have been nine feet above the ground, stood up carefully though precariously, reached up as high as I could with one hand holding up the long pole, and tried to touch the sky. After thus trying, I looked down and said to my dear child, "Honey, Daddy can't touch the sky." Of course, I couldn't touch the sky. And isn't it just as silly for a man or a woman to think they can reach all the way up to God with good works and thus merit Heaven?

God's eternal plan of salvation culminates in the Cross. Christ died there for us, and we are asked only to believe in him as Lord and Savior. This is the only way of salvation! When I graduated from college, my parents gave me a camera, and one of the first pictures I took was of the nave and chancel of Zion Lutheran Church in New Corydon, Indiana, where I served as a student pastor that summer. Shortly before I came on the scene, the good people of that congregation had refurbished their church. Among other things, to beautify the nave and chancel, they had placed a bright, new, shinny brass cross upon their altar. When I photographed that chancel with my flash attachment, the angle was such that the shiny brass cross came through as though it were on fire whereas everything else in the picture was sharp and clear. That fiery cross, blazing in prominence, has always been a parable for me of what the Lutheran Church stands for. I'm not saying that other churches don't believe this, too, but for me the centrality of this doctrine is unmistakable in the Lutheran Church. Ours is a theology which makes central and focal God's salvation.

Fourth, as Lutherans ours is a theology which ascribes preeminence and exaltation to *God's anointed*! Our theology gives preeminence and exaltation to God's Anointed. Lutheranism is radically Christ-centered. You cannot understand the Bible if you do not understand this. The first prediction of the Messiah comes already in the third chapter of Genesis. The covenant of God with Abraham in Genesis foreshadows a Savior to whom all the earth can come in faith. The prophets, again and again, looked off and out in expectation to the coming of him who would fulfill all things. Finally, "when the fullness of time had come, God sent His Son." After his death and resurrection, the apostles never tired of exalting him in sermons and epistles as the promised Messiah. What we find here in the Bible about God's Anointed is carried through in our Lutheran theology and lived out in the life of our Church.

In this we find the most distinguishing characteristic of Christianity. Our Lord and Founder, Jesus the Christ, *deliberately* places himself at the heart of our faith. Not so in other world religions. Hinduism is loyalty to an idea. Confucianism is loyalty to a tradition. Shintoism is loyalty to a particular patriotism. Buddhism is loyalty to an inner calm. And Islam is basically loyalty to a code. *Christianity alone is loyalty to a Person!* Our faith centers in and rallies around Jesus Christ as our personal Lord and Savior. We can conceive of Christianity without an organization, a liturgy, or even a creed. But to think of Christianity without Christ — that is impossible. Jesus himself said, "And I, when I am lifted up from the earth, will draw all people to myself." Such as that is not to be found in any other religion of the world. Buddha, as an example, would be utterly appalled to know that his followers sometimes pray to him. Not so our Christ who purposefully seeks to "draw all people to [himself]."

In the old Martin Luther full-length feature film of several decades ago, the Reformer has a tremendous line. There is a scene where some relics had been brought into Luther's presence, which made Father Martin quite dismayed. Later in a conversation with the vicar of the Augustinian order, Johann von Staupitz asked the young monk, "If you leave the Christian Church to live only by faith without the crutches of visible relics, what will you put in their place?" In a magnificent line, Luther answered: "Christ! Man needs *only* Jesus Christ!" Now other churches attest to that, too, as I well know, but for me the Lutheran Church carries it out better in both faith and practice. Ours is a theology which gives glory and honor to God's Anointed.

Finally, as Lutherans ours is a theology which makes gratitude and inwardness the hallmarks of the *God-inspired ethic*! Our theology makes gratitude and inwardness the hallmarks of the God-inspired ethic. Most people conceive of the Christian ethic as a long list of "do's" and "don'ts." While it is true we do have the Ten Commandments and the Sermon on the Mount, our ethic is generated rather by Someone who first does something to us on the inside. "I will put my law within them," said the Lord in today's First Lesson, "and I will write it upon their hearts; and I will be their God, and they shall be my people." Thus, our ethic is far more than law; it is a right attitude put into us by the Holy Spirit which then shines forth from the inside out. And what might that right attitude be? It is the attitude of gratitude. Without sincere gratitude to God for His many blessings and for His steadfast love, there can be no great living. As someone put it in a pithy way, "Christianity is grace and ethics is gratitude."

During the Civil War, or the War Between the States if you prefer, there was a soldier named Roswell McIntyre who deserted the Union Army. When they caught him, he was court-martialed and condemned to die. This poor soldier had no defense except to say that he was ashamed of what he had done and claimed if he were given another chance he would play the man. On the basis of that, President Lincoln pardoned him in these words: "Upon the condition that Roswell McIntyre of Co. E., 6th Regiment of New York Cavalry, returns to his Regiment and faithfully serves out his term, making up for lost time, or until otherwise discharged, he is fully pardoned for any supposed desertion heretofore committed, and this paper is his pass to go to his regiment." Thus he was forgiven his transgression against the state. Now, some might think this was moral leniency, but do not underestimate the powerful ethical motivation of gratitude. We see this clearly from what is written across the face of Mr. Lincoln's letter in the national archives: "Taken from the body of R. McIntyre at the Battle of Five Forks, Virginia, 1865." My friends, Five Forks, not far from here

— Five Forks was the last cavalry action of the war. *McIntyre went all the way through to the finish!*

Gratitude for all God's goodness, you see, goes further and lofts the Christian ethic higher than any mere lecture or moral code could ever do. Without the mainspring of gratitude triggered by faith, there can never be any great living. We are loved from on high as though there were but one of us to love. We are forgiven and declared righteous by no less than God Himself. We are assured by the Risen Christ of the Kingdom of Heaven. And we are empowered by the Holy Spirit. Thus the life we lead becomes a life of thanksgiving. Our very lives can exclaim with Saint Paul, "Thanks be to God for His inexpressible gift!" (RSV). That is where great Christian living starts. Of course, other churches say this, too, but not as often and not as loudly, I think, as our own Lutheran Church. For ours is a theology which makes gratitude the impetus of the God-inspired ethic.

This Lutheran theology of ours, which hooked me many years ago, is very important, but so also is our individual response. I conclude, therefore, with this probing thought expressed in the words of a distinguished clergyman of a bygone era. Said he, "Vital Christianity is like good music. It needs no defense, only rendition." Granted, we have a great theology and I believe the right theology, but is the music of your soul dissonant or beautiful? What kind of advertisement are you for your faith? How do you represent our congregation to the community? To be sure, we have the gospel, but then, friend, what is the gospel according to you? Remember, *vital Christianity, like good music, needs no defense, only rendition.*

Meeting God At The Corners Of Life

A New Year's Sermon for the New Millennium

Our Saviour Lutheran Church
Christiansburg, Virginia
January 2, 2000

Today, the Second Sunday after Christmas, is also by popular reckoning the first Sunday in the third millennium which marks the birth of Jesus Christ, the Savior of the world. As we pass through this significant gateway into the future, we cannot know what may lie ahead. But this we *can* know: *The Eternal God in Christ will be there to meet us at all the "corners" of life.*

Already in the Old Testament, there is much evidence of this great spiritual truth. In Psalm 46:1, for instance, we hear these emboldening words: "God is our refuge and strength, *a very present help in trouble.*" And then, "The Lord of hosts is *with us*; the God of Jacob is our refuge." These words have helped me personally through many a crisis. Further, in the Hebrew Old Testament, the actual word used for God is the word "YAHWEH" from which the familiar word, "Jehovah" comes. Literally, it means, "I am that I am." But "YAHWEH" can also be translated as though God were lovingly saying to us, "I'll be around." Isn't that comforting? Still further, in Psalm 59:10, we stumble across a seemingly uninteresting and irrelevant verse which, in the *King James Version*, reads, "The God of my mercy shall prevent me." What in the world could that mean? Well, when we learn that the word "prevent" means "go before," a better and quite accurate translation in this: "My God in his lovingkindness shall meet me at every corner." What a "blessed assurance"! Again, for your encouragement in facing whatever the future may hold, remember this word of the Psalmist: *"The Lord of hosts is with us ..."* (46:7). And do hear God saying, *"I'll be around."* And hold fast to this promise: *"My God in his loving kindness shall meet me at every corner."* There is enough here, my friends, to enable us all to stand up to anything!

As we pass into the New Testament, God's reassurance of being there gets even clearer. Before the birth of Christ at the first Christmas, Joseph heard the angel say, "...they shall call him Emmanuel, which means, *'God is with us'*" (Matthew 1:23). This being so, what is there to fear? Then, in today's Gospel, we find these empowering words: "In the beginning was the Word, and the Word was with God, and the Word was God ... And the Word" — substitute "Jesus Christ" — "And *Jesus Christ* became flesh and *lived among us.*" Here, if anywhere, is the theological meaning of Christmas. I'm reminded of a little boy, who, looking up at a picture of his absent father, said, "I wish he would step out of that picture and come down to me!" That is what happened at Christmas. God Himself in Christ left His Heavenly throne and His kingly crown and came to earth *for us!* He is thus able to touch us where we live and to meet us at all the "corners" of life.

I like the humorous little story about a group of children in a class. The teacher had become exasperated, and, just to buy a little time, she asked the children what they wanted to be when they grew up. After hearing the usual answers of lawyer, doctor, fireman, one child spoke up in an altogether different fashion. This boy, who was shy and timid, astounded the class when he said he wanted to be a lion tamer. Quite courageously, he told how he would have his whip, gun, and chair as he would face ferocious untamed lions. The class was spellbound. But when the teacher asked him how he would have the courage to do this, the child replied, "Of course, I would have my mother with me." Well, in truth, as the Scripture repeatedly asserts and as the Christmas gospel powerfully underscores, *God is right here with us to help us cope with life as we meet it at all the "corners."* "My God in His loving-kindness," said the Psalmist, "shall meet me at every corner." "Emmanuel — God is with us," said the angel. And, as we see on the face of today's bulletin, "The Word became flesh and lived among us."

We do not know what may lie ahead, but there are some "corners" which we can be sure are out there somewhere in each of our futures. Moreover, these "corners" often come upon us in contrasting entities. That is what I want to talk with you about on this first

Sunday in a new century and to reassure you as best I can that God will always be there to meet you.

First this: two contrasting "corners" to which we will all eventually come are the times of *success* and the times of *failure*. Be assured that the Eternal God will meet us at both of these inevitable "corners" of life. To somewhat misquote Kipling's classic poem titled, "If," listen to this:

> *If you can meet with Triumph and Disaster (i.e.,* Success and Failure),
> *... If you can meet with Triumph and Disaster*
> *And treat those two impostors just the same;*
> *... you'll be a* [real] *Man, my Son!* Or,
> *... you'll be a* [real] *Woman, my daughter!*

Christianity, going further, powerfully affirms that God Himself will meet us in both success and failure.

With the exception of Paul, probably the most famous missionary in the history of the Church was David Livingstone. Most people don't know, however, that his life started with failure. As a young divinity student he was asked to preach in a highland church in Scotland. When he rose to speak, he was so overwhelmed with fear that he totally forgot his text and his mind went blank when he tried to remember what he had prepared to say. He just stood there silently in the pulpit for a long while saying nothing. Then, after a lengthy and awkward pause, he simply gave up. He announced to the congregation that he couldn't preach and so stepped down from the pulpit. Well, there was an elder who, after the service, sidled up to him and suggested he was unfit to become a minister and that he ought to go back to school to prepare himself for something he could do.

God met David Livingstone in this failure, at this "corner" of his young life, and subsequently sent him in a different direction, preparing and then sending him out to Africa as a missionary doctor. More than anyone else in history David Livingstone opened up that continent in the nineteenth century through his missionary endeavors and explorations. You will recall when he dropped out of sight for several years in the mid 1860's, the whole world became concerned and a star reporter, Henry M. Stanley, was sent out into Africa to find him. You will remember when Stanley did find Livingstone in 1871, he blurted out the unforgettable words, "Dr. Livingstone, I presume!" Moreover, this heathen reporter from New York didn't escape that encounter without himself being converted to Christianity. When years later, David Livingstone died in prayer on his knees, he was so well revered that his native friends tenderly carried his body across land and sea to be buried with great honor in Westminster Abbey. None of that would ever have happened had not God met a young divinity student at the "corner"of failure one Sunday morning in a Scottish church, thus preventing him from entering the ministry.

But God also met David Livingstone at the "corner" of success. One of the times in history I wish I could have been present was a September day in 1857 when, after fifteen years in Africa, David Livingstone came back to Scotland and was invited to speak at the University of Glasgow. It was the custom of undergraduates in those days to heckle rudely the speakers that came, and those students were well prepared that day for this ineloquent missionary. They had peashooters, as any good university student had in that time; they also had toy trumpets, rattles, and noise-makers of every description. But when Livingstone walked out on that platform, those students were stunned into a respectful and reverent silence. Dr. Livingstone walked to the center of the stage with the tread of a man who had trudged eleven thousand miles through Africa. His left arm hung limply at his side, having been almost ripped from his body by a huge lion which crushed his shoulder to splinters. His face was a dark leathery brown from fifteen years in the African sun. His countenance was furrowed with innumerable lines from the bouts with African fever which had racked and emaciated his body, making him, as he called himself, "a ruckle of bones." His eyes were half blinded from being slapped across the face by a branch in the jungle. When Dr. Livingstone opened his mouth to speak that day, he apologized for his broken, hesitating speech, by informing his hearers that he had hardly spoken the English language in sixteen years.

On that historic day those students did not pull any of their customary insulting tricks, for they recognized they were in the presence of greatness. They knew that standing before them was a committed man who was literally being burned out for God. Not a rattle moved, not a foot shuffled. A hush crept over that auditorium as they listened in rapt silence to a Christian gentleman who told of the hardships and the loneliness he had been through for Christ's sake. It was in that address that Dr. Livingstone uttered these profound words: "Shall I tell you what sustained me in the midst of all those toils and hardships and incredible loneliness? It was a promise, the promise of a gentleman of the most sacred honor; it was this promise, 'Lo, I am with you alway, even to the end of the world.' " When this servant of the Lord, who couldn't preach a sermon, had finished speaking that day, far from being disrespectful, those same students, who had come to heckle, some with tears in their eyes, rose up spontaneously to give this saint of God an emotional and lengthy standing applause.

What is success? What is failure? Are they not, as Kipling said, "impostors"? And are not *both* success and failure among the hardest things we have to deal with in this life? But be assured, my friends, that God will meet you at these two "corners"and then see you all the way through them! This can happen, I maintain, because at that first Christmas Mary "brought forth her firstborn son, and wrapped Him in swaddling cloths, and laid him in a manger" (KJV) and "... the Word became flesh and lived among us."

Now secondly: as we face the future, we had better be prepared for two more contrasting "corners" which are inescapable — namely, weakness and strength. Though personally I have generally been strong and healthy, early on in my ministry I became so weak and sick that I was sent to Mayo's Clinic and then spent three months in bed during which time I thought I was dying. But the God I preach about in Church has always been there to meet me both in weakness and in strength.

The late Catherine Marshall was the wife of probably the most distinguished Chaplain ever of the United States Senate, Dr. Peter Marshall, then pastor of the New York Avenue Presbyterian Church in Washington. Following his sudden death in 1946, Catherine

Marshall became a writer of distinction. In her autobiography titled, *Meeting God at Every Turn,* she has an inspiring chapter titled "Illness" in which she describes two years of being bedfast in their Washington parsonage with tuberculosis. Catherine Marshall skillfully wrote in this chapter about how God came close to her during this time to teach her patience and obedience and to give her insight into the Scripture and spirituality. She also described what she called "the most real and vivid experience of (her) life." Listen!

> *In the middle of the night I was awakened. The room was in total darkness. Instantly sensing something alive, electric in the room, I sat bolt upright in bed. Past all credible belief, suddenly, unaccountably, Christ was there, in Person, standing by the right side of my bed ... Jesus was smiling at me tenderly, lovingly, whimsically — as though a trifle amused at my too-intense serious- ness about myself. His attitude seemed to say, "Relax! There's not a thing wrong here that I can't take care of."*

Her healing began at that moment, and Catherine Marshall emerged from that experience a stronger Christian. I cannot guarantee that in sickness you will see Christ as she did. I cannot guarantee that you will become well as she did. But I *can guarantee* that God will meet you in the experience of sickness, take you by the hand, up- hold you with His presence, and teach you great spiritual lessons.

We need to remember here, too, that Saint Paul was sick, and whatever physical ailment he had, it did not go away. He tells us in 2 Corinthians 12:7 that he had a "thorn in the flesh" which, almost certainly, was a physical infirmity. Scholars have speculated that this "thorn in the flesh" could have been recurring bouts of malaria or, perhaps, frequent migraine headaches. Whatever this physical ailment might have been, the apostle got down on his knees and besought the Lord *thrice* to rid him of this debilitating ailment, but the answer he received from the Lord was not wellness but this: "My grace is sufficient for you, for my power is made perfect in weakness" (2 Corinthians 12:9). That was not a healing, but it was a *strengthening*. So he could later write to the Romans, as I think it is best put in the King James Version, "We then that are strong ought to bear the infirmities of the weak" (15:1).

Now some people aren't too good at handling their strength, but the apostle was! Writing to the Philippians, he said, "I know how to be abased, and I know how to abound" (4:12 KJV). One half of that passage is not at all surprising. He says, first, that he knows how to be "abased," that is, sick, hungry, poor, or downtrodden. He is thus testifying to the familiar fact that Christ gives to people faith, steadiness, and power to confront various forms of hardship including illness. But then, he says, "I know how to abound." He writes of *that* as though it were a difficult affair. He is saying, you see, that he has learned how to use his superior strength in the service of others. To be sure, some people are ruined or made bitter by sickness and adversity, but I suggest there are even more people who become arrogant in their strength and health as though they were somehow superior to those less fortunate. They then fall on their faces over the precipice of their own well-being. Not Paul! He knew "how to abound." Hear the great apostle as he tells the Corinthians all he had to endure to live a serviceable life in the advancement of the Kingdom of God. He writes of

> ... *far greater labors, far more imprisonments, with countless floggings, and often near death. Five times I have received from the Jews the forty lashes minus one. Three times I was beaten with rods. Once I received a stoning. Three times I was shipwrecked; for a night and a day I was adrift at sea; on frequent journeys, in danger from rivers, danger from bandits, danger from my own people, danger from Gentiles, danger in the city, danger in the wilderness, danger at sea, danger from false brothers and sisters; in toil and hardship, through many a sleepless night, hungry and thirsty, often without food, cold and naked. And besides other things, I am under daily pressure because of my anxiety for all the churches.* — 2 Corinthians 11:23-28

My soul! How did the man stand all that? Not altogether well and, further, being frequently blind-sided, harassed, and persecuted by real enemies Paul, nonetheless, used such strength as the good Lord chose to give him in being of service to others. He knew "how to abound."

Paul thus used his strength to "bear the infirmities of the weak." This happened because the Lord God Almighty met him at that "corner" of his life. So he could write, "Whenever I am weak, then I am strong" (2 Corinthians 12:10). Moreover, in the end, Paul could cry out in a triumph born of faith in the ever-present God, "I have fought the good fight, I have finished the race, I have kept the faith" (2 Timothy 4:7). This is the sort of thing which happens because that first Christmas on a Bethlehem hillside an angel chorus sang, "Glory to God in the highest ..." as "... the Word became flesh and lived among us."

Now finally to two more contrasting "corners" which, I suspect we all meet daily. They are the temptations of sin and self-righteousness. Part of our human predicament is that we must contend with both of these problems. Something within us must again and again cry out with that publican in the Temple, "God, be merciful to me, a sinner!" (Luke 18:13). Or, perhaps more appropriately, "God, be merciful to me, *a fool!*" There was, however, another man that day in the Temple who prayed thus, "God, I thank you that I am not like other people" after which he went on to remind God of how good he was. All of us have a publican within, but all us have a Pharisee there, too. We are tempted by both sin and self-righteousness, but what I am saying now is that the Living God in Christ is right there, not only to meet us, but to rescue us at both of these dangerous "corners" of life, either of which can destroy us.

Sin, of course, is *the* fundamental problem of humankind. It ruins so many things and brings so many people, including church members, down to destruction. And we must all face it. One of our fine and saintly Lutheran seminary presidents once said that, "... the badness has not all drained out of me, nor all the meanness and evil thoughts." That is authentic and real, isn't it? Saint Paul said as much when he cried out, "Wretched man that I am!" (Romans 7:24). And not for nothing do we repeatedly confess in this church "that we are in bondage to sin and cannot free ourselves," whereupon we then lay out before God that, "We have sinned ... in thought, word, and deed," not only "by what we have done" but also by "what we have left undone." At the end of this path, *uninterrupted by Christ's presence and saving grace,* lies death and destruction.

But enter the Church where the Lord God Himself meets us week by week in worship. One of my seminary professors wrote, "The Christian fellowship is by its very nature a covenanted group of weak, sinful, and needy persons." That we are, aren't we? On the first day of the week, my friends, we regularly meet together as a "fellowship of those overtaken in faults." And Christ meets us through clergy such as I, saying, "As a called and ordained minister of the Church of Christ, and by his authority, I declare to you the entire forgiveness of all your sins." In our service, our songs, our sermons, and our sacraments God meets us here and speaks in various ways these comforting words: "Your sins are forgiven." So we are thus *able* to "go in peace" to "serve the Lord."

But something else again happens here in Church. The Lord attacks our self-righteousness, which is also sinful, and now and again he gives us a good humbling. The Good Lord in our midst is fully able to burst our bubble. Sometimes he sears us with a burning revelation of Truth, saying, in effect, "You shall know the Truth, and Truth will make you *mad!*"

As a pastor I have always tried to take seriously the prophetic side of the ordained ministry, that is, *to afflict the comfortable* as well as to comfort the afflicted. Years ago, as an example, I began a hard-hitting sermon on sin with these words: "This is no time for a jelly-bellied, lily-livered sermon." One parishioner, who considered herself a few cuts above the rest of us, came to me afterward and said sarcastically, "We've had good ministers in this church before you (implying that I was not in that select company), and they didn't preach about sin like you do." I replied with a smile, "Maybe they just didn't know the subject as well as I do!" In time, that woman became my friend, and I visited her grave only a couple of years ago. Another time I had a naughty Sunday school teacher who ran away from her home. She tried to minimize her own responsibility by haughtily pretending to be a victim. I tracked her down to an apartment in Atlantic City and went to see her. While talking to her, I became totally exasperated with her intransigence, and suddenly — was it God prompting me? — I got up and said to her emphatically, "We're all free to go to hell in our own way." Then I left slamming the door behind me. I am happy to say that she was back in church and Sunday school the following week. Another time, I believe in a church council meeting, I stated that I think it is a sin to die without leaving at least something behind to the Church of Christ. Well, there was one self-centered church member who lit into me belligerently for that statement, but not long thereafter a good man died, and, having heeded my words, left $40,000 to the church. In such times and many others as well, I was much strengthened by these words God spoke to Jeremiah: "They will fight against you; but they shall not prevail against you, for *I am with you*, to deliver you" (15:20).

Thus, God meets us in church and in life even though some of us be clergy. Through the Holy Spirit He reveals to us the sinfulness of our sin; He also pierces our self-righteousness but then God brings to us the incomparable spiritual blessing of forgiveness through Jesus Christ, the Savior. This took place because that first Christmas in "the fulness of time" Wise Men knelt down to worship the newborn King as "the Word became flesh and lived among us."

This true story comes out of World War I. There was a British soldier who watched his close friend go out from the trenches in those terrible days into what was called "No Man's Land." He saw his friend hit with a bullet and fall whereupon he said to his officer, "Sir, he's my friend. We've been very close. Can I go out and bring him in?" The officer said, "No, of course you can't. Look at the fire that is going on out there. Nobody could live out there. Your friend is mortally wounded, and if you go, you'll be mortally wounded too, and I'll lose both of you." But before the officer had finished speaking, the man was off, and the officer could only watch. Somehow that hero got his friend onto his shoulders and he staggered back with him into the home trenches, but his friend was

166

dead, and he himself was mortally wounded. The officer, who was very angry and upset, said, "I told you! I told you it wasn't worth it. He's dead now and you're mortally wounded, just as I said." The hero looked up into the officer's face with his dying eyes and said, "It was worth it, Sir." "Worth it," said the officer. "How could it be worth it?" Then the dying man spoke these poignant last words: "It was worth it, Sir, because when I got to him he said, 'Jim, I knew you'd come. *I knew you'd come.*'"

So long ago in "the little town of Bethlehem" God in Christ came and "the Word became flesh and lived among us." Consequently, you can enter the new millennium *safely,* and you can stride into the future *confidently,* for the Lord God Almighty will always be around to meet you at the "corners" of life.

Praise My Soul, The King Of Heaven

A Sermon for Christ the King Sunday

St. Mark's Lutheran Church
Charlotte, North Carolina
November 26, 2000

Good morning! I want you to know that I am very pleased to be with you here today in St. Mark's Church. In this I am reminded of a Transfiguration hymn in the old *Common Service Book* which begins, "'Tis good, Lord, to be here!" I'm saying that I deeply appreciate this opportunity to see and rejoice with you on the completion of the splendid renovation and expansion of your church facilities. I'm also glad to spend some precious time here with former parishioners, friends, and relatives, and to stand once more in this pulpit where so many spiritual giants have stood before me. Yes, "'Tis good, Lord, *really good* to be here!" Thank you, good people, for inviting me.

This is especially true in my case because, I must tell you, that at least five times in bygone years your senior pastor, my brother-in-law, almost completed my earthly journey *prematurely*, and, of course, dead men don't stand in pulpits to preach sermons. Twice on trips with Peter, for example, I became fatigued and asked my dear brother-in-law to drive the car a while so that I could sleep in the front passenger seat. Unfortunately, my dozing off was so suggestive to Peter that he, too, went to sleep — *at the wheel*. In so doing, he drove the car off the road at a high speed, which both of these times suddenly awakened us in terror as we were being shaken around violently, even hitting our heads on the ceiling of the car. It's a wonder that we didn't roll over when your pastor tried to get us back on the road! Another time we rented a wooden rowboat to take a ride on Devil's Lake in the Wisconsin Dells. We didn't notice as we started out that the boat was wet on the bottom, but we did notice out in the middle of that so-called bottomless lake when the water started pouring in uncontrollably and we began to sink.

169

My wife Mary and I bailed the water out as fast as we could, which wasn't fast enough to keep ahead of the rising water, while Peter rowed with all his teenage might, which wasn't powerful enough to move that rickety old boat anywhere. As we were actually going down into that chilly lake water where there was no bottom, still some distance from shore, I seem to remember Peter saying, forgetting my wife was a woman, "I guess it's going to be every man for himself." That wasn't too comforting! Instead of giving up, however, I waved my long arms wildly, and, fortunately, some people in a motorboat some distance away came to us, thinking I had either lost my mind or we were in real trouble.

Worst of all, back in the '50s, we accepted an invitation from some of my parishioners in northern Illinois to go boating with them on the Pecatonica River. They had what they called a "pumpkin seed boat," which is one of those small, flat speedboats that climbs out of the water, planes off, and then really goes seemingly, with only the motor in the water. Well, Peter noticed how the rest of us would easily turn around in that fifty-foot-wide river by slowing down and then gunning the boat so that it slid around and started going the other direction. When Peter's turn came, he approached the turn at full speed and could not turn the boat around. In the process, believe it or not, he climbed a tree with that boat. Yes, there was a fallen tree there where he had intended to turn around, and he took that speeding boat right up into the branches with the motor still running wildly in the air at full speed. I walked toward him in the shallow water, not quite knowing what to do. I knew I couldn't stop the propeller with my bare hands; I knew also that this small boat could suddenly dislodge from its perch, come at me, and kill me. Still I approached this accident intending somehow to help, as Mary trembled in the fear that she would lose us both. At this point, mercifully, God intervened and stopped the motor. I think the good Lord was saying under his breath, "I've got to save those two guys from themselves so that one day they can both serve as senior pastors in St. Mark's, Charlotte." I could also share with you the time I foolishly accepted an invitation from Peter to go horseback riding, but that is just too painful a story to tell. These were all scary experiences, though perhaps a bit exaggerated, and I do want you to realize fully how grateful I am to be here, *alive and well.*

I must, however, quickly add that Peter and I have had many, many more good times together when we were safely enjoying one another's company. Peter is more than a brother-in-law to me; for decades I have considered him the brother I never had. Moreover, I admire him as a person and a pastor in the Church. I also rejoice in the successes of his leadership in this congregation and how, together with the splendid staff and the faithful lay people of this church, you have reached another notable milestone in your history in this recently completed building program. May God continue to bless you as you move ever forward in your remarkable witness and service in the Kingdom of God.

Today, as you know, is Christ the King Sunday. In our Second Lesson from the first chapter of Revelation God speaks some words which in the last chapter of Revelation Christ makes his own, saying, "I am the Alpha and the Omega, the first and the last, the beginning and the end" (Revelation 22:13). Then in today's Gospel we hear Pilate asking Jesus, " 'So you are a king?' Jesus answered, 'You say that I am a king. For this I was born, and for this I came into the world' " (John 18:37). Add to that these words from Revelation where we are told that Christ "on his robe and on his thigh ... has a name inscribed, *'King of kings and Lord of lords'* " (Revelation 19:16). Christ the King, that's what I want to talk about this morning as I lift up for you some pertinent phrases from a great hymn we will be singing at the conclusion of this sermon — namely, "Praise, My Soul, The King Of Heaven."

I

First these significant words are embedded in that hymn: "Praise the everlasting King!" It stands written in God's Word that "the kingdom of the world has become the kingdom of our Lord and of His Christ, and he shall reign forever and ever" (Revelation 11:15). Therefore, "Praise, my soul, the King of Heaven" we shall be singing, "Praise the *everlasting* King!" Let me see if I can make these words come alive.

171

When I was a sophomore in the university, my professor of English literature asked me one day in class, "Mr. Boye — that's how they spoke to us in those days — Mr. Boye, tell us which of the great English poets, Byron, Shelley, or Keats, do you like the best?" I paused to measure my words carefully, and then gave him an answer he didn't want to hear. "To tell the truth, Professor," I said, "I don't like any of the three." I don't suppose that answer helped my grade. But there is, nevertheless, one poem of Percy Bysshe Shelley with a strange name that has stuck in my mind all these years. Shelley called it simply "Ozymandias." In this poem a traveler comes upon a ruined statue of an ancient pharaoh way out in the middle of nowhere in the sands of Egypt. This pharaoh, known as Ozymandias, had boasted during his life of all his great achievements, but now centuries later, almost nothing remains of him or his legacy. On the pedestal of that ruined statue, therefore, these telling words appear:

> My name is Ozymandias, king of kings:
> Look on my works, ye Mighty, and despair!

Nothing remains, you see, but in contrast our Lord Christ is truly for time and eternity "King of kings and Lord of lords." So we shall be singing in the sermon hymn, "Praise the everlasting King!"

Shortly after history tumbled out of B.C. into A.D., there stood in the city of Ephesus a magnificent temple of the goddess, Diana, that looked like it would be there forever. That heathen temple was considered one of the seven wonders of the ancient world. Not for nothing, therefore, did those Ephesians cry out, "Great is Diana of the Ephesians." At this same time in history there was also a very ordinary hall in Ephesus, belonging to a man named Tyrannus, where people called "followers of his way" came together. In this rented lecture hall, a little bald-headed Jew with fiery eyes and winsome zeal named Paul shared with them the Good News of Christ the Savior.

In time, so the Bible tells us, a riot ensued between these "followers of the way" and the devotees of Diana. Those screaming Ephesians could not be silenced for two whole hours, and thus they made enough noise and threatened enough terror that Paul left

172

the city, and the Church of Ephesus had to go underground. I suspect that very night the word that echoed back and forth in the streets of Ephesus was this: "We're done with those troublesome 'followers of the way' now. We will hear no more from them."

How wrong they were! What appeared to be eternal, the temple of Diana, turned out to be temporary; and what appeared to be temporary, the Church of Jesus Christ, turned out to be eternal. You can travel to Ephesus now and see where that temple of Diana once stood, but all you will see is a single reconstructed column and large stones scattered in a stagnant, smelly swamp, inhabited by frogs. Nobody worships Diana now, and nobody cares. But the Church of "the everlasting King," Jesus Christ, now girdles the globe with the message of salvation.

> O where are kings and empires now,
> Of old that went and came?
> But, Lord, Thy Church is praying yet,
> A thousand years the same.

But did not Christ the King tell us as much when he said to his disciples, "... upon this rock" [meaning faith in Christ] — "upon this rock I will build my church, and the gates of hell shall not prevail against it" (Matthew 16:18). So today, on Christ the King Sunday we sing appropriately, "Praise the *everlasting* King!"

II

Now consider these further words from that hymn: "Praise him for his grace and favor." Jesus said, as the translation runs in *The New English Bible*, "My grace is all you need." So, "Praise my soul, the King of heaven," we shall be singing; "Praise him for his *grace and favor*." Let me see if I can make these words unforgettable.

Far be it from me to fault the search committee that brought me to this pastorate twenty years ago, but now that I am not candidating for a church anymore, I must tell you what these good folks missed. Well intentioned as they were, they utterly failed to look into my roots. Had they done so, they would have run across

173

one of my ancestors, Jens Henrik Boye, who was born in the same month as I only 105 years before me. I hold in my hand a biography of this famous Danish man, and it isn't even the only recent book written about him, even though he has been dead now for well over 100 years. Jens was both smart and talented. He painted portraits of people and wrote ballads. He was also very well liked and became quite a successful merchant. Children loved him, and there was something about him which made the pretty girls want to sidle up to him. But alas, Jens went bad and became a criminal, turning his intelligence and his very considerable talents into the despicable "profession" of crime. But, I must tell you, Jens was no ordinary criminal. He had quite an operation going. He actually organized a sizable armed gang, the listing of which takes up four full pages in this biography. He needed such a gang to help him in all his robberies, his assaults on innocent people, setting arson blazes on property, and the lucrative business of counterfeiting. When they caught him the first time and put him in prison, he was clever enough to escape and continue his life of crime. In the end, he murdered a farmer during a burglary. He was again arrested, put in prison, tired, and this time condemned to die. Jens Henrik Boye, my ancestor, was therefore beheaded over a century ago near the town of Assens, Denmark, where my cousin still lives. The sword that beheaded Jens is still on prominent display in a major museum in Denmark. When Denmark outlawed capital punishment, Jens Henrik Boye had the dubious distinction of being the last one to go. Now, this man was actually one of my ancestors, and your search committee didn't search enough to find this piece of history in my background. I might add, parenthetically, that I suspect another search committee probably didn't ask Peter, either, about ol' Cal Setzer? Anyway, hold on to these facts about Jens for a bit and let me tell you something else.

There is a novelist named David Bender who wrote a book titled, *The Confession of O. J. Simpson*. The writer of this intriguing and thought-provoking work of fiction asks the question, "What might have happened if O. J. had admitted his guilt, confessed his crime, apologized to the Brown and Goldman families, and become an altogether different man?" Doesn't it excite the imagination even to contemplate such a thing? Could O. J., perhaps, have become a *real Christian* and witnessed to his faith in Christ as his Savior and King? Do you think such a thing is impossible?

Listen! My ancestor, Jens Henrik Boye, also a famous criminal, actually did all these things and much more. It is no idle happenstance that interesting biographies are still being written about him in our generation. His contemporaries were stunned by the profound change in this criminal, and none who saw his remarkable conversion doubted his sincerity. His contemporaries were utterly convinced that his conversion was authentic. Jens became a deeply repentant and religious man who studied the Scriptures and prayed, even leaving some of his prayers behind in writing such as this: "Oh, God," he prayed, "I am a sinful soul, and I have broken Your holy law, 'Thou shalt not kill' ... Oh! Savior, free my sinful soul and ... cleanse me in your blood and mercy ... O Jesus, crucified for me ... your suffering upon the cross all worldly sins did cover." What a remarkable story it would have made if O. J. had prayed from the heart like this! Moreover, there is good theology in this prayer, even though it was prayed and penned by a criminal on death row. Not only that, Jens also wrote beautiful letters of apology asking for forgiveness from those whom he had so terribly wronged. And this gifted but previously misguided man wrote a hymn, from which I wish to quote the last two verses:

> Lest now my prayer, oh gracious God,
> For Jesus' sake reach unto You.
> Oh! free me from the snares of sin,
> In mercy hear my pleading.
> O let the door of Heaven be
> Unlocked and open unto me
> My soul and spirit to enter.
>
> In peace I bow to You my God.
> I turn to You in mercy
> I know You promised Your love
> To send Your Holy Spirit to me,

And when my head and body are divided
In Your Eternal City,
I will find Your grace.

Jens Henrik Boye was beheaded on August 16, 1856. He was peaceful and cooperative to the end, and as he knelt to receive the fatal blow, his last calm and confident words of faith were these: "I commend myself to God." To this day, that place of execution is known as "Boye's Hill." And why not? His life and death illustrate so compellingly that of which we sing in the hymn, "Amazing Grace." This true story shows how far "the grace of the Lord Jesus Christ, the love of God, and the communion of the Holy Spirit" (2 Corinthians 13:14) will stretch. And let these words of another hymnist be now etched into your souls, never to be forgotten, that, "... the love of God is broader than the measures of our mind." Well do we sing, "Praise him for his *grace and favor.*"

III
Now finally on this Christ the King Sunday how ought we respond to this amazing Christ? The sermon hymn suggests a powerful answer in the first verse: "To his feet your tribute bring ... Alleluia! Alleluia!" Recall again Jesus' words in our text: "I am the Alpha and the Omega, the first and the last, the beginning and the end." So we can praise him in the words of the Psalmist, "... even from everlasting to everlasting, you are God." Therefore, "Praise, my soul, the King of heaven," we shall soon be singing, "To his feet *your tribute bring.*" Let me see if I can make these phrases start to vibrate through the marrow of your souls.

In the motion picture version of Lloyd Douglas' great novel, *The Robe*, there is a tremendous line charged with emotion and packed with conviction. These words are spoken by Marcellus, the Roman tribune who had been given the distasteful task of crucifying Christ and the two revolutionaries. These arresting words appear in the story after Marcellus had been haunted for some time by his possession of the seamless robe of Jesus that he had won by gambling beneath the Cross. His stirring utterance is the maturation of an earnest man seeking to know if Jesus was all that

176

his disciples had said he was. At last the full impact of the person of Jesus Christ, "the King of kings and Lord of lords," fully masters Marcellus as he lays his tribute before him, saying, oh so magnificently, "From this hour forward, I pledge to you my sword, my soul, *my life.*" Have *we* thus surrendered to Christ? Friends, "To his feet *your tribute bring.*"

The best tribute any of us can lay at Jesus' feet is *ourselves.* Saint Paul wrote to the Church at Corinth, "I seek not yours, but you" (2 Corinthians 12:14). The apostle carries this thought further, writing to the Romans, "I appeal to you, therefore, brothers and sisters, by the mercies of God, to present your bodies as a living sacrifice, holy and acceptable to God, which is your spiritual worship" (12:1). The Lord Christ, you see, though not disinterested in our time, our talents, and our treasures, is *primarily* interested in our surrender to him as Master and Lord of life. He wants us, knowing full well that once we bow down our lives to him in uttermost surrender, he has everything else as well. And where might we end up? Luther told us in these words: "If anyone would rap at the door of my heart and ask, 'Who lives there?' I would answer, 'Martin Luther once lived here. But Martin Luther has moved out, and Jesus Christ has moved in!' " That is what it means to lay your tribute at Jesus' feet until at last the candle of life flickers out.

Ere we finish, I would like to share with you something quite personal, which I hope I will not regret saying. Hear me well! Though not certainly, but very probably, *this is the last sermon I will ever stand in a pulpit to preach.* For a variety of reasons, I just don't think I am going to be able to do this anymore. But that's all right. It is awesome to have been called by God into the gospel ministry in the first place, and in addition to that, the Lord Christ has given me such a long run at it. But now I think it is time to lay down the mantle of preaching. At 72, of course, I shall continue to serve "my King, my Savior" in other ways as long as I have life and strength.

You might be interested to know that I preached my first sermon in June of 1948, some 52 years ago, interestingly at another St. Mark's Church, this one in Clayton, Missouri. For more than a half a century now, I have tried my best to do that which the Lord long ago charged Isaiah (52:7) to do — namely, to announce peace, to bring good news, to proclaim salvation, and to say to the people, "Your God reigns." Not infrequently through these years, I felt the Holy Spirit enabled me to preach "over my head," and, "... strengthened in [my] inner being with power through [the same] Spirit" (Ephesians 3:16), I was challenged to do far more in my ministerial career than I could ever have imagined when I began. But now, to misquote Ecclesiastes somewhat, I do think "there is a time to start preaching, and there is a time to stop." I think that time is now, and if that be the case and if this is indeed my final sermon *ever*, what a day to go out on: Christ the King Sunday!

Let me add perspective now by recounting a slice of history I have shared with you before. There was in the second century a frightful martyrdom in the city of Smyrna during the time that a man of some note named Statius Quadratus was the provincial governor or proconsul, as they called such an official in that day. During his time, the aged bishop and saint, Polycarp, was brought to trial. The hostile judge pointed his finger and cried out at the saintly Polycarp, who stood innocently before him, "You are to renounce the faith! You are to curse the name of Christ!" But Polycarp, as you will remember, gave this inspired answer: "Fourscore and six years have I served him, and he never did me wrong: how can I revile my King, my Savior?" Outraged, the government under Statius Quadratus dragged Polycarp to the amphitheater in Smyrna and burned him to death. But the young Church in Smyrna hurled its defiance in the face of his murderers; for when later it came down in the annals of the Church what happened, it was careful to put in the precise date of this historic event, which it noted in this way: "Statius Quadratus, proconsul; *Jesus Christ, King forever!*"

Likewise, Richard Boye, and add to that the pastors of this congregation, Peter Setzer, Michael Ward, Monta Maki-Curry, Jay Harbinson — pastors and preachers in the Church for one brief moment between eternities, but *JESUS CHRIST, KING FOREVER!* Alleluia! Amen!

Postscript

From a post-retirement sermon on Christian Ethics:

There is no way back to where you started out from, so take each step along life's pathway thoughtfully and carefully. When you make a choice, always consider where the swift current of that choice may eventually sweep you. To make life's pilgrimage safer, take the Church and the Church's Lord very seriously lest you end up morally bankrupt and spiritually dead. Listen carefully to and evaluate the advice and counsel of parents, friends, and mentors lest you fall into self-destructive ways. Refuse to permit yourself to become a victim of life lest you sink deeper into that pit and then find it harder to climb back up to maturity by taking responsibility for your own life. Keep a good attitude toward others and toward life itself lest good people begin to shy away from you and you become isolated. When you suffer adverse circumstances, for you surely will, always take the high road out lest you end up where you do not want to go. These guidelines faithfully followed will not necessarily lead you to success, health, and constant happiness, but I can promise you this: you will be able to live with yourself; you will be able to look yourself in the mirror without shame; and you will live a significant life that counts.

A slightly revised older prayer of blessing for confirmands which can well serve as a daily prayer:

> *Dear Father in Heaven, for Jesus' sake, renew and increase in us the gift of the Holy Spirit, to our strengthening in faith, to our growth in grace, to our patience in suffering, and to the blessed hope of everlasting life. Amen.*